WHAT PEOPLE ARE SAYING ABOUT
THE ENERGY OF BELONGING

"A highly practical workbook, *The Energy of Belonging* offers a vast array of simple, actionable ideas to help people develop genuine connections at work. It's a how-to-guide for building relationships based on respect and caring that foster engagement and belonging at work."

—Amy C. Edmondson
Novartis Professor of Leadership, Harvard Business School;
author of *Right Kind of Wrong:*
The Science of Failing Well and *The Fearless Organization: Creating*
Psychological Safety in the Workplace for Learning, Innovation, and Growth

"Connect. Respect. Protect. Those are the magic words to create a culture of belonging. Wendy does a spectacular job of helping us understand what each means and how to implement actions that deliver on their promise. She is an expert at providing plenty of reasons to increase Belonging, backed by research giants such as LinkedIn, Gallup, HBR, McKinsey, Amy Edmondson, and others. But that's not the most essential reason for this book's excellence. Its brilliance lies in the seventy-five practical, 'implement 'em now' actions you can take to make a difference today. Her personal touches and stories will make you laugh aloud and cry with compassion.

"If you want to implement something that makes a big difference with a little effort, look no farther. You've found the answer. Take action today to help your colleagues feel valued and welcomed as a part of your team, department, company, or social group. *The Energy of Belonging* is certainly the best book I've ever read to help yourself, your colleagues, and your organization to create a culture of Belonging. Reading it gave me dozens of instant ideas and ready-now actions to take. Put this book in the winner's circle and on your reading list today."

—Elaine Biech
2022 ISA Thought Leader, author of #1 Bestseller,
The Art and Science of Training

"Wendy Gates Corbett's words inspire us to embrace our own role in fostering belonging, both within ourselves and among others. This is a must-read for anyone interested in changing their workplace culture."

—Melissa Daimler
Author of *ReCulturing* and Chief Learning Officer, Udemy

"It's all about the A's in Wendy Gates Corbett's *The Energy of Belonging*: authenticity, actionability, and 'aha!' moments. With authenticity and vulnerability, Wendy walks readers through seventy-five actionable steps anyone can take to meaningfully shift their workplace culture towards a greater sense of belonging for all. While they're cleverly simple and often subtle in execution, make no mistake—these ideas are designed for maximum positive impact!"

—Kade Kimber
President, Harmony NC LGBT+ Allied Chamber of Commerce

"As someone who spent five transformative years at Zappos, I wholeheartedly endorse Wendy Gates Corbett's *The Energy of Belonging*. I can genuinely say that the book resonates deeply with my experiences. It captures the essence of fostering a workplace community where every voice is valued and cherished, making it a must-read for anyone seeking a supportive and cohesive work environment."

—Mike Williams
CEO, Chief Community Builder, and bestselling author of
Doing to Done

"In *The Energy of Belonging*, Wendy Gates Corbett takes a fresh and innovative look at community building by focusing on what individuals can do for others in creating the place we all love! The '*connect, respect*, and *protect*' framework makes it easy to remember and follow. I can't wait to start applying some of the example ideas in the book with our team."

—Luis Morales
Executive Director, Duke University's Master of
Engineering Management Program

"In *The Energy of Belonging*, Wendy Gates Corbett unveils how the complex nature of belonging can be shaped by every employee throughout the organization through deliberate but simple actions towards each other within our daily interactions. She makes the seemingly hard work easy."

—LaPonda J. Fitchpatrick
SHRM-SCP, ACE, ASC, EDICT©, IDI®

"In a world craving connection, *The Energy of Belonging* emerges as a beacon of hope, compassion, and practicality. Wendy Gates Corbett invites us all to embark on a journey that promises not only a deeper sense of belonging but also sparks a richer understanding of what it truly means to create a workplace community. This is a must-read for anyone transforming their workplace culture!"

—Mary McNevin, Ed.D.
Executive coach and talent advisor

"Discover the power of belonging with Wendy's transformative '*connect, respect,* and *protect*' framework. Navigate disagreements without assigning blame—a challenge global societies grapple with. Delve into this guide and witness profound changes in yourself, your teams, and your communities. A game-changer that's urgently needed!"

—Justin Jones-Fosu
Author of *I Respectfully Disagree: How to Have Difficult Conversations in a Divided World*

"Before Wendy Gates Corbett wrote this book, I watched how masterful, thoughtful, and focused she was one-on-one and in groups about how each voice meant something to her. To now see in words what she already embodied excites me. How people act in the small gestures matters to me, and the way Wendy Gates Corbett brings this into practical applications at work is thrilling. The impact of this book will transcend barriers to communication and help create a culture of safety and support."

—John M. O'Connor
President, CareerPro Inc.

"We all benefit when we have healthy workplaces where we know we will be supported and where we can do our best work. But in the hustle of life, it's easy to rush past interactions that created this desired state. Wendy Gates Corbett's informative and deeply authentic book equips managers and others with stories from the front lines and practical steps to take so that 'belonging' can become both an action verb and outcome in your workplace."

—Allegra Jordan
Duke University Adjunct Associate Professor of Leadership & Management, Pratt School of Engineering

"Wow, I *so* wish my boss had had this book! This fresh guide to building belonging would have saved me countless coffees and endless confusion over whether or not I was valued at my Fortune 100 job in the entertainment industry. I'm so glad today's workforce can have the resource that's highly needed and long overdue: this practical, fun, and welcoming guide to fostering community and connection on every team at every organization. With its actionable ideas, robust insights from 1,500+ professionals, and easy-to-apply framework, *The Energy of Belonging* is undoubtedly the spark you've been looking for to increase retention, drive results, and most importantly, help everyone do their best work together by being their most authentic selves."

—Annie Franceschi
Author of *Establish Yourself* and founder of Greatest Story Creative®

"Wendy Gates Corbett knows how to make people feel that they *belong*. She is an established leader in the DEIB space, and reaffirms her knowledge, expertise, and heart in *The Energy of Belonging* with valuable research from people and reported resources. The stories she shares offer eye-opening perspectives from the lenses of people from various backgrounds and their own challenges. It can be difficult for us to know that things we say and do breed negative outcomes. Wendy professionally calls us out and invites us in to explore how we can incorporate more inclusive behaviors and language to improve every relationship so we can *connect, respect,* and *protect* each other as we are with our differences. Well done!"

—**Cindy Tschosik**
Writer, editor, and author coach

"The Energy of Belonging is a positive book for people who want to improve their workplace. Wendy Gates Corbett explains how important it is for everyone to feel like they belong at work. She shows when people feel like they're part of a team, it helps grow confidence and increases productivity. Gates Corbett explains how to make this feeling of belonging happen. She tells stories about how leaders and workers can work together to reach their goals. She says making people feel valued and connected is like an art. She also asks employees for their ideas on how to make this happen. In the book, Gates Corbett shares her own experiences and stories from others, making the idea of belonging real and powerful. She helps readers learn how to make their workplaces better. Through *The Energy of Belonging,* Gates Corbett shows us how to make our workplaces more connected and happier. She gives us lots of cool ideas to make our teams stronger. Gates Corbett's work reminds us that amazing things happen when people feel *connected, respected,* and *protected."*

—**Pegine**
Leadership speaker, recognized as one of the largest
minority-owned businesses in Northeast Florida

"If you care about your workplace culture, this book is for you. Yes, this is a must read and reference tool for any organizational leader and HR professional, but it's also for anyone who genuinely cares about where they work and wants to do their part to foster inclusion at work. Through real-life stories, readers broaden their perspective and gain valuable insight. Readers also gain practical, doable, and meaningful tips for intentionally creating a culture where everyone matters. As Wendy Gates Corbett illustrates in *The Energy of Belonging,* it doesn't take a lot of effort, and these small actions create big positive shifts in the culture."

—**Dawn Sander**
Founder and principal, DPS Leadership LLC

THE
ENERGY
— OF —
BELONGING

75 Ideas to Spark Workplace Community

WENDY GATES CORBETT

Publishing support provided by
Ignite Press
5070 N. Sixth St. #189
Fresno, CA 93710
www.IgnitePress.us

ISBN: 979-8-9892352-0-9
ISBN: 979-8-9892352-1-6 (E-book)

For bulk purchases and for booking, contact:

Wendy Gates Corbett
wendy@signature-presentations.com
www.wendygatescorbett.com

Library of Congress Control Number: 2023916471

Cover design by Usman Tariq
Edited by Elizabeth Arterberry
Interior design by Jetlaunch

FIRST EDITION

To my family and Don:
I've always known to the depths of my soul that I belong with you.

ACKNOWLEDGMENTS

First and foremost, to my husband, Don: thank you for your unwavering faith in me. Your love was the sustaining energy that fueled me across the finish line that is this very book. From your daily and sometimes hourly support to reading for "Belonging" vs. "belonging," your love is a primary spark.

To my family—Mom, Dad, Todd, Tim, Keith, Lorraine, Grace, Dustin, Jesse, Tyler, Roxy, Forrest, Tristan, Jiana, Ava, Andrew, Jack Henry, Westyn, Derrick, Mike, Denise, Ana, Roland, Jalen, and Cameron—thank you for believing in me.

Cindy Tschosik, my editor, writing coach, dear friend, and Silver Sister: this book would simply not be what it is without your magic, your expertise, your guidance, your love, and your faithful voice. From the initial outline stages to our conversation about the book title, you've guided me with fierce love for me and my message. Thank you, Cindy.

To the Ignite Press team, including Everett O'Keefe, Zelda Fogle, Malia Sexton, and Elizabeth Arterberry: thank you for your patience and perseverance in bringing this book to life. Through all the 'life' that happened since Day One, you were with me every step of the way.

Melardz Vee (a.k.a. "Mel"): for seven years (and counting), you have brought my messages to life with your incredible design abilities. Thank you for your fantastic wizardry in translating my fuzzy ideas into beautiful, meaningful, and powerful imagery.

Marcy Venezia and Mark Sanford: we are three peas in the group coaching program pod Cindy created for us. Our 8:00 AM writing sprints gave me the momentum needed to get started and get finished!

Pegine Echevarria, my coach, my mentor, and dear friend: from your supportive nudge to embrace my research and title of "belonging researcher" to your innate ability to guide me in discovering "the Energy of Belonging," I would not be the leader I am today without your expert combination of gentle and powerful guidance.

My Silver Sisters, Cindy Tschosik, Annette Fazio, and Jennifer Einolf: who knew (besides Pegine) that saying "yes!" to becoming a Silver Sister would lead to such a beautifully nourishing friendship and mastermind? Your love and cheers were and are essential to my well-being.

Thank you to the professionals who graciously gave their time and permission to share their candid stories of belonging (and not): Dr. Mira Brancu, Chris Coladonato, Don Corbett, Michael Grant, Melony Johnson, Kade Kimber, Ronda Moore, Luis Morales, Samantha P., Marcey Rader, Brian Sakofsky, Dawn Sander, Johnna Sharpe, and Elizabeth S. Your stories helped make the impact of belonging and exclusion real and palpable.

Thank you to the 1,500+ employees who responded to the *Belonging at Work Survey*©. Your insights will help readers grasp their own power to foster belonging in their workplace communities.

To my clients: I am filled with gratitude and appreciation for the honor of working with you and your team members to explore your own expanding understanding. This is hard work, and it demands reflection and vulnerability. Thank you for going into this delicate space with me.

I am thankful for all of my coworkers, colleagues, and work BFFs from all of my work and volunteer experiences. You've taught me the importance of workplace community.

I save a special *thank you* for you, dear reader! I appreciate your interest in exploring how you can foster belonging in your environment. You can. And I have no doubt you will!

TABLE OF CONTENTS

LETTER FROM THE AUTHOR

WELCOME,
I'M SO GLAD YOU'RE HERE

Many of us, including me, have had experiences where we felt like we didn't belong. My guess is that you're reading this book because you've had a similar experience. We carry those feelings into adulthood and into workplaces. I've been moved by how many employees struggle with a sense of belonging at work. Can you relate? At the same time, it's astonishing how many employees feel trapped watching those colleagues suffer in their struggle. In my search for solutions, I found a gap in the belonging resources available for employees. That gap compelled me to write this book. I hope it sparks ideas for you.

—Wendy

ABOUT THE AUTHOR, WENDY GATES CORBETT

The Impetus to Empower Employees to Spark Change

Working with organizations on training, talent development, and behavioral change, I witnessed hundreds of employees lacking a sense of belonging in their workplace. They didn't feel important, appreciated, or safe to express themselves. Doing research was not part of my initial plan. I simply wanted to know which types of specific employee behaviors led employees to feel as though they belonged in a workplace community. I assumed the answers were out there somewhere; I just needed to find them. When I couldn't find them, I wondered why, and I set out to answer two questions:

QUESTION #1:
"Which employee actions and behaviors contribute to a sense of belonging in workplace communities?"

In my search for answers, I devoured every piece of existing research that I could find from thought leaders like Amy Edmondson, the professor of leadership and management at Harvard Business School, and Adam Grant, the professor of management and psychology at The Wharton School. I have deep respect for both of them as they are experts on workplace culture. I read books, articles, and whitepapers on what contributes to feeling cared for at work from The Center for Creative Leadership, Gallup, Josh Bersin, Coqual (formerly the Center for Talent Innovation), and BetterUp. The short answer to the question is: "many factors contribute to a sense of belonging at work." There's a longer answer, too.

While there are numerous factors that contribute to a caring workplace community, I discovered three themes that appeared consistently. For employees to feel a sense of belonging at work, they need to feel:

- *Connected* to their peers, their leaders, and the organization.
- *Respected* by their peers and colleagues.
- *Protected* or safe to fully express who they are and use their voice.

These three themes form the foundation of my Belonging framework.

Connected

to the people we work with, our leaders, and the organization

Respected

by the people we work with and our leaders

Protected

by the promise that we are safe to be and to express ourself freely

Great! First question answered:

> For employees to feel they belong in their workplace community, they need to feel connected, respected, and protected.

The answer to Question #1 led me to ask:

QUESTION #2:
How do we do *that*? How do employees *connect* with, *respect*, and *protect* their work BFFs and colleagues?

I found most of the existing answers to this question targeted senior executives, HR professionals, managers, and team leaders. There was a void in answers geared towards employees. Since I couldn't find any answers that focused on employee behavior, I decided to do my own research to find out.

I've been in workplace communities where I felt invisible. I've also been the employee who was desperate for ideas to re-engage my disengaged work BFFs (best friends forever) to show them that they are respected and valued, and to create the kind of environment they wanted, where they felt safe, seen, and heard.

My desire to equip employees at all levels with ideas they can use to build belonging is an alignment of my personal journey of belonging with my professional journey into organizational culture. I am fired up to make building a workplace community that people love "doable" for those who don't have the time, budget, or a five-year strategic plan to change the culture in their organization.

I am all about effective, simple, "low-hanging fruit" kinds of solutions that can be easily added into what employees already do. Most of the professionals I know don't have the extra time or the budget to devote to building the thriving workplace community they want, but they are hungry for ideas they can use as early as tomorrow to make a positive difference.

The ideas in this book are not guaranteed to cause huge organization-wide culture shifts. Instead, they empower individual employees to make small and significant changes in their workplace communities one interaction at a time. They spark lots of small wins that gather momentum, and these can spark big changes that produce a thriving workplace community.

Channeling My Education and My Superpowers

I pursued a master's degree in industrial/organizational psychology in the late 1990s to feed my fascination with what and who shapes an organization's culture and how it happens. Expanding my focus to belonging at work was a natural next step from my personal journey of understanding that concept, as you will read about in Part One.

The process of formulating the ideas in this book for sparking workplace community called on three of my superpowers, which involve inspiring big wins from small actions:

1. Twenty years ago, my graduate studies of organizational psychology lit a spark that motivated me to continue learning about employee engagement and psychological safety at work.
2. My journey to becoming a leader in the training industry fine-tuned my ability to distill complex material into easy-to-understand language and practical, actionable skills. I present and write in ways that make behavior change attainable through easy integration of concepts into everyday life, which is also key in being an impactful and effective professional speaker.
3. As an adjunct professor at Duke University, I engage my instructional and program design prowess to break down behavior change into bite-sized actions to show my students how they can integrate new behaviors in their environment using their existing skill set.

For over twenty-five years as a training and talent development executive, I've designed and facilitated thousands of programs. My clients consistently say they appreciate my knack for providing simple actions that don't take more time or money and are based on skills they already have. They say I make the overwhelming not only doable, but feasible and fun. That's my goal with this book: to make building Belonging at work doable and fun using skills employees already have.

Kade is a colleague and a client who has hired me several times as a keynote speaker to present about Belonging. Here's what he said when I asked him why he continues to hire me:

Testimonial from Kade

"As humans, it's inherent in our nature that we complicate things. We imagine them to be much more complex than they really are. It's so easy to overlook the simple, 101-level ideas. Having them pointed out to us is eye-opening. Wendy, you bring it down to earth and that, to me, is where the difference lies. That is how you stand out."

ABOUT THE BOOK

The Purpose of This Book

The purpose of this book is to empower and equip employees at all levels with specific, simple ideas they can use to help their colleagues who feel disconnected, dis- or not respected, and/or not safe to express themselves. *The Energy of Belonging* is filled with ideas that employees can use to help their colleagues feel connected, respected, and protected in their workplace communities. The ideas presented are not rocket science—in fact, they're the polar opposite of rocket science! They are intentionally simple.

This book demonstrates how employees can build an energized, productive, fun workplace community by:

- Deepening their sense of connection to their colleagues and their organization.
- Showing others they are respected.
- Ensuring their coworkers are protected by trusting relationships.

The Book Structure

The Energy of Belonging is divided into seven parts. The framework is as follows:

Part One: A bit of my backstory regarding Belonging.
Part Two: The definition of Belonging explains my definition.
Part Three: The Energy of Belonging describes the concept.
Part Four: How to *connect* to peers, leaders, and the organization.
Part Five: How to show *respect* to peers and leaders.
Part Six: How to *protect* colleagues by creating a safe, trusting environment.
Part Seven: Summary.
Parts Four through Six include:

- Examples of the specific behaviors that help employees feel *connected*, *respected*, and *protected* that are drawn from over 1,500 survey responses.
- Personal stories about belonging and exclusion from professionals in various industries.
- 25 simple ideas employees can use to:
  - Connect: Build a deeper connection.
  - Respect: Act in ways that say, "I respect you and value your talent."
  - Protect: Create an environment where everyone feels safe and included.
- Sparks to assist and encourage you in reflecting on your own experiences with belonging at work.

How to Use This Book

The framework elements *"connect, respect,* and *protect"* are related, but they are not linear. You can jump around the chapters and explore them in any order. If you're eager to get right to the seventy-five ideas for sparking workplace community, go directly to:

- **25 Simple Ideas to Spark *Connection* at Work** in Part Four
- **25 Simple Ideas to Show *Respect* at Work** in Part Five
- **25 Simple Ideas to *Protect* Your Colleagues** in Part Six

PART ONE

YOU DON'T BELONG HERE!
YOU'RE DIFFERENT!

You Don't Belong Here! You're Different!

I was five years old the first time Laura said to me, "You don't belong here! You're different!" She was my seven-year-old next-door neighbor. I was different from her because I'm biracial, I'd been adopted by a white family, and we lived in a white neighborhood. Laura and I were friends who split our time between being best friends and fierce enemies (often on the same day).

"You don't belong here! You're different!"

I internalized these words in my soul. I believed them so deeply they became my guiding belief for thirty-five years. I believed, *if you think I'm different from you, then I don't belong.* I lived in a constant state of fear that my "differentness" (my word) would be discovered, which would leave me feeling excluded and all alone. My deeply rooted fear and belief controlled how I behaved and engaged with others for the next thirty years: all throughout school, in my careers, and into my early forties. In middle school, my survival instincts went into overdrive, and my chameleon persona was born. In each personal interaction, the chameleon persona's job was to convince you that I was the same as you: smart (or not), athletic (or not), driven (or not). I was a perpetual imposter, being everyone but myself.

At work, in the very place where I developed and expressed my professional identity, I was afraid to be truly seen or heard because I was terrified my "differentness" would be revealed. I stifled my voice and avoided being the first to state my opinions, ideas, or recommendations. I couldn't risk a difference of opinion; I was too afraid of the consequences. As a result, I was seen as a supportive team player and a cheerleader, but not as a leader. My false belief also hindered genuine connection with my coworkers because I hid my true self from them. I never expressed the real me. I always tried to be like them so that I would "belong."

"You don't belong here! You're different!"

The words rooted themselves deeply within me. Fortunately, with growth, grace, persistence, and lots of self-work, they are no longer a guiding belief. I work ruthlessly to conquer this fear, and today, when it whispers in my ear and tries to hijack my self-confidence, I refuse to give it air most of the time (I'm a work in progress). I've learned to confront it by employing strategies which give me the energy to reconnect with my personal sources of strength, power, and love. I no longer hide or remain silent when I have something to say. I am no longer afraid of my "differentness." I cherish my real relationships and genuine connections with my colleagues. I am respected for what I bring to the table, and I feel safe to be fully me without fear of being excluded. My work life is thriving.

I know the impact I am making in the world, and through sharing this book with you, my reader, I hope you find the answers you seek to help you embrace the Energy of Belonging so that you and your coworkers will feel more *connected, respected,* and *protected.*

The Impetus to Belong (and Why I Wrote This Book)

As human beings, we have an intrinsic need to be included. Belonging is essential to our well-being. Yet, many of us are unaware of our own power to influence whether people around us feel as though they belong. This is especially true in schools, in our social circles, and in our workplace environments. We feel ill-equipped to embrace and practice Belonging, as well as to extend it to others, because it is a nebulous concept. Between my own traumatic emotional turmoil from feeling that I did not belong and witnessing the prevalence of how the lack of belonging infiltrates the workplace and our world, I was compelled to author this book. Just like learning essential communication skills to be successful selling products and services, as well as a successful member of a team, we need to be aware of and knowledgeable about how each of us has the power to contribute to a vibrant, supportive workplace community culture, one where everyone feels *connected, respected,* and *protected.*

A Missing Spark: Uncovering the Giant Gap to Belong

As I prepared to write this book for my organizational consulting programs and for keynote presentations, I was eager to learn about the specific, tangible employee behaviors and actions that foster belonging in workplace communities. I assumed someone had already identified them, so I sought to find them. As I reviewed existing resources and research, I found resources targeting the C-Suite, human resources professionals, and other organizational leaders, but I couldn't find any resources for the everyday employee. There was no support for the people on the shop floor, in the cubicles, and on Zoom for those who worried about their workplace BFFs, for those who agonized over their colleagues who were disengaging and/or leaving because they felt disconnected and disregarded. I couldn't find books, blogs, or podcasts for employees who wanted to do **something positive** for their coworkers.

I easily could have written a prophetic business case for "why organizations should build belonging in their workplace," but my passion for the topic made me yearn to go beyond *organizational* change, towards empowering *individual* change for the benefit of whole organizations. The information I found wasn't surprising, but the repercussions of the lack of a sense of belonging in the workplace were astounding.

DID YOU KNOW?

59% of employees are "quiet quitting"—putting forth minimal effort because they feel lost and are psychologically disconnected from their workplace community.[1]
—Gallup, 2023

Imagine the success and engagement an organization could have if they weren't contributing to this statistic!

There's a good reason to "do something" about belonging because it's directly linked to employee retention, which is a key focus for both employees and employers today. The 2023 Gallup State of the Workplace Report announced that "53% of workers around the world think the job market is rich and ripe for those who are looking to leave their employer."[2] If companies want to improve employee retention, then it's time to spark something more to create workplace communities where BFFs want to stay. This book is for employees who want to help the coworkers they care about and contribute to creating a place they (and their work BFFs) love. It provides seventy-five ideas those employees can use to spark belonging in their own environment.

Build Belonging with Employees First

Before an organization commits to building Belonging in the workplace, we need to start with the basics: recognizing how all employees play an essential role, have the power to enact change, and can build belonging from the ground up. I'm not saying that everyone has to love everyone they work with; that isn't realistic. However, inviting people to feel they belong doesn't demand love. It requests civility and human kindness regardless of our personal feelings towards our coworkers.

The Energy of Belonging is not intended to convince readers of the value of belonging at work. Its goal is to provide practical, tangible ideas employees can use to create a connected, respected, and protected workplace community. Throughout, I offer my findings from salient research and insights from notable experts, a few of my own life experiences and lessons, and seventy-five simple ideas for action to provide readers with insightful perspectives and to offer them adaptable actions that promote and instill a workplace culture that *connects*, *respects*, and *protects*.

PART TWO

BELONGING DEFINED, EXPLAINED, AND DEMONSTRATED

The Definition of Belonging

Belonging is an emotion and an outcome of human interactions, as is exclusion, which is the opposite of Belonging. Ronda's story below demonstrates the influence other people's actions can have on our own sense of belonging at work.

"He patted me on the head and said, 'You done good, girl.'"

"I built out an inaugural multi-day leadership development program for employees on the path to partnership. I worked really hard for months pulling it together. It was a huge success. During the closing ceremony on the last day of the program, the managing partner for whom I have a lot of respect acknowledged me from the stage and everyone applauded me. I was feeling amazing! I was feeling on top of the world because the program was a hit, I could see the impact the program had, and my months of hard work had paid off.

"One of the partners who was a member of the core team I worked with on this project came up to me. He patted me on the head and said, 'You done good, girl. You done good.' I was *shocked*. I'd just been recognized for all of my hard work, and I was on Cloud Nine. And he just diminished it by patting me on the head and calling me 'girl.'

"I remember getting on the plane and crying the whole way home. At a time when I should have been elated, I was completely deflated. I brought my A-game and left it all on the field and that was his response? I was so discouraged."

—Ronda

Definitions of Belonging vary widely. This didn't surprise me, since it's such an indistinct concept. We tend to have our own personal definitions of belonging, in part because, as a feeling or a sense, we each experience it uniquely. We know it when we feel it (or don't), but it's challenging to define. The myriad of definitions I found seemed incomplete, so I created my own:

> Belonging is the sense of security and support that results from feeling welcomed, valued, accepted, and safe, that we are a part of something meaningful that's larger than ourselves.
>
> —Wendy Gates Corbett

Belonging is an outcome: the result of how people behave towards each other. It is created by human interactions that make others feel seen, valued by, and safe with the people around them.

What Belonging Is and Is Not

Belonging Is	Belonging Is Not
• An outcome • Created by human interactions • Based on behaviors • Accepting others' imperfections	• Complicated • Limited to leaders to create • Policy-driven • Judging others' weaknesses

Landing on a definition of belonging provided me with a new sense of clarity and focus. The definition served as a beacon, shining brightly and guiding me in the right direction. This was the next step in my journey to answer the question, "**Which employee behaviors contribute to a sense of belonging in workplace communities?**" I had this burning need to know the actions employees can take to help their colleagues feel welcomed, valued, and safe. I couldn't find answers in existing resources, so it led me to my research.

Five Facts: How Belonging Impacts the Workplace

DID YOU KNOW?

Belonging is the #2 driver of great work cultures.

—LinkedIn's 2022 Workplace Learning Report

Morale, momentum, and productivity all suffer when talented colleagues disengage or leave the organization. All employees can play a role in tackling disengagement, reducing turnover, and ensuring others feel connected, respected, and protected. Both Belonging and exclusion, the opposite of Belonging, have organizational consequences. Consider these five facts about Belonging:

1. Research from BetterUp found that employees who felt they belonged took 75% fewer sick days than those who did not feel like they belonged.[3]
2. We don't work alone. In fact, data shows that the time we spend in collaborative activities has increased more than 50% in the last 20 years.[4] Belonging influences our ability to collaborate effectively.
3. As companies shift from siloed models to an ecosystem model, collaborative work with cross-functional groups will only increase. However, as many as 75% of cross-functional teams are dysfunctional in multiple areas, including alignment with company goals and clear-cut communication.[5]
4. Exclusion in a workplace community impacts team performance as well as individual performance. BetterUp's study

found that in a team environment, individuals who feel excluded are less willing to contribute a concerted effort to benefit the team. Exclusion influences productivity, too: employees who feel excluded can be 25% less productive.[6]

5. According to LinkedIn's 2022 Workplace Learning Report, Belonging is the #2 driver of great work cultures, which makes it a critical area of development for organizations worldwide because it impacts their bottom line.

Drivers for Great Work Culture from LinkedIn

1. Opportunities to learn and grow
2. **Belonging**
3. Organizational values
4. Support for well-being
5. Collaboration[7]

Five Facts: How Exclusion Negatively Impacts the Workplace

There are personal consequences when employees feel like they don't belong. In my own experience, when I felt excluded by my colleagues, my workdays (and weekends) were fraught with anxiety. Work felt like trudging through neck-deep mud. I dreaded booting up my computer in the morning. When I saw the *"Available"* status on my colleagues' Skype accounts, it felt like a cruel joke because they didn't seem "available" to me. I actually had a visceral negative reaction to logging into Skype: it created a toxic pit in my stomach because seeing the list of my coworkers made me feel even more isolated, excluded, and shut out.

Five Actual Consequences of Exclusion as Told by Interviewees

1. I eventually disengaged by keeping my microphone muted and my camera off in team meetings. I contributed as little as my natural drive would let me because I felt excluded.
2. Melony stopped offering to stay late to train staff on the night shift when she realized she was the only person on her team who her boss never invited to team lunches.
3. Chris, a remote employee, cc'd a senior leader on an email and asked why remote employees were never invited to the all-hands meeting at headquarters where food, drinks, and swag flowed freely.
4. Mira left her job believing she wasn't cut out for her role because her boss made her feel like an outsider.
5. Kade stopped traveling to his corporate office and chose to work from home instead because his colleagues never invited him to join their conversations.

Eventually, we all left those organizations and took our talent, passion, and contributions with us.

A Gap in Belonging Resources for Employees Sparks New Research

There is a place for discussion of theory, research, and the historical foundations of Belonging, but this book is not that place. I prefer to focus on actionable ideas that can be implemented tomorrow, so the ideas for building belonging to follow are simple and practical. You can try one tomorrow because they don't require a lot of time, effort, or money. The ideas only require you to have a desire to do something to build belonging wherever you are.

Doing research was not part of my initial plan. I simply wanted to know which types of specific employee behaviors led employees to feel as though they belonged in their workplace community. I assumed the answers were already out there somewhere; I just needed to find them. I took a multi-pronged approach as I scoured resources in search of simple, everyday actions that contribute to belonging at work, which resulted in several findings:

- I found policies for HR professionals.
- I found transformational culture initiatives for organizational development experts.
- I found strategies and even KPIs for executives and leaders.

What I could not find were actions at the employee, peer, or team member level. So, I initiated my own qualitative research project to identify specific and tangible answers. My research project included a literature review, designing and administering a survey (the *Belonging at Work Survey*©), and conducting interviews.

My research approach can be summed up in one word: *ask*, as in "ask employees what their colleagues and leaders do that make them feel like they belong." The overarching research question I continuously strive to answer is:

"Which specific employee behaviors and actions contribute to employees feeling *connected*, *respected*, and/or *protected* in a workplace community?"

The *Belonging at Work Survey*© was designed to gather specific examples of behaviors that make employees feel *connected*, *respected*, and *protected*. The anonymous survey consists of seven open-ended prompts (see example survey prompts and responses below).

I asked employees these questions in two key ways:

1. Via the *Belonging at Work Survey*©, which resulted in more than 1,500 responses at the time of this publishing; and
2. One-on-one interviews with professionals in a variety of industries and positions that explored their experiences with

belonging (or not) at work. Stories from the interviews are included throughout the book as real-world examples demonstrating the incredible impact, as well as how to *create* or *destroy* "belongingness" one person (or action) at a time. The interviews offered more in-depth perspectives of how they felt they belonged (or not) and how it impacted them.

**SAMPLE OF THE BELONGING AT WORK SURVEY©
PROMPTS AND RESPONSES**

In the *Belonging at Work Survey©*, we use prompts such as these to solicit responses:

"I feel connected to my colleagues when they…" "Invite me to join their conversation."

"I feel respected by my colleagues and leaders when…" "They ask me for my opinion."

"I feel unprotected at work when…" "I hear my coworkers gossiping about other employees."

SHARE YOUR EXPERIENCES!

If you would like to complete the *Belonging at Work Survey©*, the link is: https://bit.ly/3LcGUBe

Thank you!

It Only Takes a Spark to Build Community

Responses to the *Belonging at Work Survey©* identified the "what," as in "what behaviors contribute to belonging at work," and the "how," as in "how do individuals contribute to belonging at work?" As I examined the survey responses, I developed a list of the most common actions that respondents said made them feel *connected*, *respected*, and *protected*. The answers I found were surprising, though not surprising in their simplicity. For example, one of the most common responses was **"I feel respected by my colleagues and leaders when they thank me for my contributions."** We took the behaviors identified by the survey (i.e., "when they thank me for my contributions") and generated ideas for ways to make those behaviors happen. Using this response, we generated ideas for how to thank colleagues more often. In many cases, like this one, the idea was an obvious no-brainer.

Survey Prompt	Response	Idea Generated from Response
"I feel respected by my colleagues and leaders when..."	"...they thank me for my contributions."	Tell a colleague what you appreciate about their contributions to a recent project.

All throughout the 1,500+ surveys, suggestions were offered. Time and again, employees weren't recommending grand gestures. They offered ideas for simple acts that employers and coworkers could do that would "spark" a burst in camaraderie, energy, and collaboration. I was inspired and felt affirmed in my belief that, if I could share these sparks with you and employers, then, collectively, we could make an enormous impact on employee engagement, retention, and organizational success.

As you read through this book, you will see that each part covering *connect*, *respect*, and *protect* includes twenty-five ideas to spark and build community, trust, and respect in the workplace. We often hear, "it takes a village to build community." In this case, what we are aiming to accomplish is to build Belonging in our workplace communities. From the 1,500+ people who responded to the survey and the people I interviewed, I've learned that it just takes a simple, doable "spark" of action to make people feel like they belong!

Read Ronda's story below for an example of the positive impact your action can have even in a delicate situation.

"They risked being awkward to show me they cared."

"In the days and weeks after the murder of George Floyd, I had a number of colleagues reach out to check on me. They saw what was happening on the national and, eventually, the global stage and recognized that I was a member of the Black community. They responded to the cues they saw and inquired about my well-being. I know it must have felt awkward for my colleagues, because they didn't know what the right thing to do was in that situation. But I really appreciate that they thought of me as someone they knew who was part of a community that was hurting, and they did what they felt they could do at the time—check in on me. They risked being awkward and made an effort to reach out to me and show they cared."

—Ronda

Belonging Begins with Employees First

The focus of this book is on individual employees, but that doesn't mean the organization and its leaders don't play an important role in building Belonging. Organizations play a critical role in creating a foundation of Belonging in the way they set and live up to their core values, through the policies they implement, and what metrics matter to them. In fact, according to Coqual (formerly the Center for Talent Innovation), a global non-profit think tank consisting of DEI executives and leaders, all levels of the organization influence the sense of Belonging.[8] Table 1 summarizes the common ways organizations build Belonging at different levels.

How Belonging Is Built at Different Organizational Levels (Adapted from Coqual)[9]

Table 1. How Belonging Is Built at Different Organizational Levels

Organization Level	Organizations create the foundation of Belonging through whether and how well they actually: • diversify top leadership positions. • enfold diversity, equity, inclusion, and belonging (DEIB) priorities into succession efforts. • measure and give rewards based upon key performance indicators (KPIs). These foundational behaviors determine whether employees see role models and people who look like them advance within the company.
Senior Leadership	Senior leaders set the tone and expectations for all behavior at work, including those that: • foster belonging. • set and reinforce clear expectations that employees feel valued as part of their job. • model the behavior they desire in their company.
Managers	Managers foster a community of belonging when they: • demonstrate to their direct reports that they are valued, welcomed, and included. • provide recognition, attention, and feedback on a day-to-day basis, not just via performance evaluations.

Peers	Peers can:
	• provide an essential supportive community for colleagues. • advocate for self-care and well-being. • provide peer-based recognition.

All levels of the organization contribute to a sense of Belonging, but, the behaviors that build belonging are performed by individuals, hands down. Ultimately, Belonging thrives or fails at the employee level for two reasons:

1. Belonging is naturally formed through human interactions.
2. Behavior change happens at the individual level. Regardless of organizational policy and KPIs, the simple actions employees take to connect with their colleagues, show respect, and create protected workplace communities cannot be mandated.

Belonging thrives or fails
at the employee level

Belonging Beyond the Workplace

Building Belonging outside of work is also an important initiative, and each spark makes a difference regardless of the environment. Contributing to others feeling seen, heard, and valued can also be applied with family, friends, volunteers, spiritual or religious communities, and within professional or industry associations—and let's not forget the professional and personal development opportunities we take part in each year. Ultimately, my goal is to fill your pockets with ideas you can use to build Belonging in all of your communities. Can you imagine a school, work lunchroom, or playground where everyone feels that they are welcome and they Belong?

Outside of my workplace, one of the most powerful team experiences I've ever had was in a volunteer leadership role as a member of the National Advisors for Chapters (NAC) for the Association for Talent Development (ATD), an international organization for corporate training professionals. NAC is a team of former chapter presidents who support approximately 1,200 volunteer chapter leaders around the United States.

NAC was a significant time commitment, sometimes requiring ten to twenty hours per month, in addition to our responsibilities at work. Even so, whenever a NAC team member asked for help, there was always a bunch of people willing to assist. The chairperson, ATD staff, and team members fostered a community where:

Connected

- We invested time in team-building activities to get to know each other.
- We dedicated time in each meeting for members to share significant moments in their lives.
- We often infused humor and laughter into our time working together.

Respected

- Our unique talents were appreciated.
- Our career and development goals were supported.
- We made sure every person had an opportunity to voice their opinion before decisions were made by consensus.

Protected

- We made a commitment to communicate openly and honestly.
- Mistakes were not held against us.
- We were safe to be ourselves (at our best and at our worst).
- It was safe to take risks, even if our ventures failed.

As a result, I felt like I belonged. Although we were volunteers and a virtual team, we developed a solid mutual commitment, we were reliable, productive, innovative, and successful. We had the psychological safety and trust that allowed us to say, "I've got a project going on at work. I could use some help with my chapter leader meeting this month." We also had the trust to share, "I've been laid off from my job. If you have any contacts at Acme Company or know of any positions available, please let me know." We supported and cared about each other. Our meetings were fun, energizing, and productive. I loved being part of that team!

When was the last time you felt as though you belonged; *truly* belonged? Have you ever noticed how excited you get when you do feel like you belong in a community? Do you have a higher energy level, or smile more broadly? While writing this book, I recognized that during the times I feel I belong both within and outside of my career, I experience an ethereal level of giddiness. I can't wait to get going with my BFFs. I jump out of bed with *enthusiasm*. I want to work harder because I'm *enjoying* the work I'm doing, the difference I'm making, and the people who surround me. That level of energy does not exist when I feel excluded, ignored, unvalued, or irrelevant. When I don't belong, and others don't belong, that energy is missing. We don't jump out of bed with enthusiasm. We don't enjoy the work we do, and we don't work harder. We aren't making a difference, and we are excluded and isolated. The culture depletes all of our energy to the point where we don't have any to give.

As we will see in the next section, "the Energy of Belonging" is the spark that infuses our entire soul when we feel we belong, and the rewards are infinite.

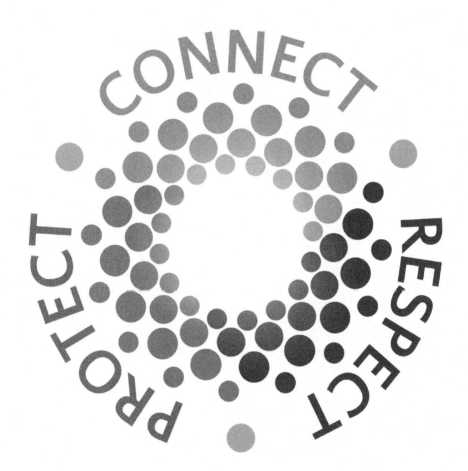

PART THREE

THE ENERGY OF BELONGING

"We're being acquired."

I Didn't Know How Good I Had It

The announcement shocked me. I'd worked at Learn.com for six years when we were acquired by Taleo. After the acquisition, I was relieved and grateful that I still had my job. Unfortunately, Art, my boss of six years, didn't get to keep his.

In my first meeting with my new boss, Chuck, he said, "I know you've been through a lot with this acquisition. I know that you and Art were close. How are you doing with all of this change, Wendy?"

It was a real question, and I could tell he was genuinely interested in my response. I appreciated that Chuck acknowledged my feelings and the loss that I'd experienced. I was grieving a trusted relationship. Chuck's thoughtful inquiry created a welcoming—and welcome— connection that would then be reinforced by the other members of this team I had just joined.

I Was Connected, Respected, and Protected

One of our first responsibilities as a new leadership team was to merge two teams, two sets of processes, and two different approaches to client services to determine our path forward. The way we determined this new path showed our respect for one another's knowledge and experience: we created a list of processes and each director described how their team handled the assignment, sharing the good, the bad, and the ugly that arose from each. We shared what worked well and candidly shared the challenges. For each process, we decided as a team whether to adopt the Taleo approach, the Learn.com approach, or come up with a new way. What could have been an exercise wrought with vulnerability turned out to be one that was energizing, motivating, and fun. We had a blast as we collaboratively optimized our processes and charted a plan for our path forward. It felt like we were solving a giant puzzle. Throughout the experience, we developed into a cohesive team that had fun as we worked hard together.

Together, we created a safe space to admit the flaws and weak points in our processes. We fostered an atmosphere of trust by respecting each other's input, insights, and opinions. As a result, I quickly felt connected to my new team members, including my new boss. I was part of a team where my experience and knowledge were valued. I felt comfortable acknowledging the shortcomings in the training business and processes I'd help build at Learn.com. I respected my colleagues and didn't judge their weaknesses.

We gelled even as a virtual team. We worked together easily. Our work was fun and productive because our ideas and energies fed off each other. We worked and played well together. We cared about each other. I became friends with my team members. I belonged on this team. This is when I recognized the power of "the Energy of Belonging."

On Chuck's team, I knew I belonged because…

- I discovered the value of trusting, deeper relationships at work.
- I experienced the creativity and productivity possible when colleagues and direct reports know they are valued and respected.
- I realized the generative power of workplace communities where it is safe to be flawed and to produce imperfect outcomes.

My experience on Chuck's team wasn't surprising. Close work friendships create healthy workplace communities and foster a sense of belonging. Numerous studies have shown that having close work friendships increases productivity because friends are more committed, they communicate better, and they encourage each other.[10] In 2015, the International Social Survey Program confirmed the substantial positive impact that work friendships can have on job satisfaction in the Harvard Business Review article, *"The Power of Work Friends."*[11] In fact, in the twelve domains of workplace quality, it ranks first in terms of explaining the variation in job satisfaction. Gallup's 2022 study found that workplace friendships also impact employees' likelihood to recommend their workplace to others and their intent to leave.[12] This leads me to my next workplace experience, which was not as positive as my time on Chuck's team.

And Then I Was Invisible

I didn't realize how important the senses of connection, respect, and safety at work were until they were glaringly absent in another role at a different company. I joined this organization in the first global role created by one of the founders. I was eager to meet my new colleagues, to learn about them and their positions. I couldn't wait to brainstorm with them to identify the ways I could help them. Based on my experience as a part of Chuck's team, I had high hopes that this would be another high-energy, high-fun workplace community.

With the anticipation of being the new kid in school, I introduced myself to my new colleagues. I explained my role and gave them a heads-up to look for an invitation for a one-on-one meeting to get to know each other. My meeting invitations went unanswered or were declined with no explanation. My emails were ignored. During my first trip to the England office to spend time with my colleagues in person (my first time in England), I was left to explore London by myself. I felt abandoned and excluded. I was invisible.

What was I doing wrong? I felt like a failure, questioning my own competence. I felt inadequate and started to doubt my ability to build rapport. Did I make a mistake taking this role? I felt dismissed and disregarded by my coworkers' silence. I felt like an outsider, as if no one at this company even cared that I was there.

I desperately yearned for a coworker to say, "Hi, Wendy! I'm glad you're here," or for a colleague to explain, "here's how our process works." I wished someone (anyone!) would show interest in me as a human being. I wanted to be welcomed as a member of the team with talents and skills that would make their jobs easier. However, I couldn't do that alone. I needed their help.

One of the few people who did help me was Lilly.

Lilly helped me as best she could. She was one of the colleagues I connected with the most while I was there. Lilly worked in the England office. She responded to my emails and answered my questions. Lilly could see I was struggling with how standoffish most people were. "I'm sorry, Wendy. I wish there was something I could do to help. It's just how we are." I struggled for nine months to connect with my colleagues and wriggle my way into their workplace community.

Eventually, I stopped trying to force my way into their circles. I gave up and left the company. I felt dejected, but I also felt really bad for Lilly because she witnessed my unsuccessful efforts to gain entry to their workplace community. She didn't know what to do and she felt powerless to help me. It didn't have to be that way. What could she do?

What can any employee do in Lilly's situation? Feeling powerless drains us of vital energy. Working in an environment with disengaged and disconnected colleagues is draining, too. Belonging is fuel, and creating it is a power we all have. This book provides more than seventy-five ideas for employees, like Lilly, who have colleagues they care about who:

- feel disconnected from their coworkers.
- feel their talents, skills, and contributions are not valued or appreciated.
- don't feel safe to use their voice.

What Is the Energy of Belonging?

**"Belonging is the fuel for employee and
organizational success."**

—Achievers Workforce Institute, 2021

Belonging is the sense of security and safety that results from feeling welcomed, valued, accepted, and safe as part of something meaningful and larger than ourselves. It is a multiplier of engagement, productivity, and creativity, as the energy it generates not only fuels these things, but also inspires higher overall performance and better quality problem-solving. Glint's research found that employees who feel they belong are six times as likely to bring their best selves to work and do their best work.[13] Additional insights come from O.C. Tanner, a company that provides a suite of employee recognition tools. From an organizational perspective, O.C. Tanner's 2023 global culture report confirms that a sense of Belonging positively relates to retention and satisfaction with employee experience, estimated tenure, and job satisfaction.[14]

When the Energy Is Present

"The Energy of Belonging" is the outcome that results from the degree of Belonging in a community. When Belonging is strong among the members of a group or team, there is positive energy produced; this can be seen in the positive outcomes we discuss throughout this book. The vibe among the members of any group fuels cohesion, creates momentum, and produces positive results. Like my experience on Chuck's team, together, we were a well-oiled machine getting great work done. It's like a symphony orchestra, where each instrument contributes to a beautiful piece of symphonic song—the music wouldn't be the same without one of those instruments.

Think about a healthy, cohesive team you were a part of that really gelled: you felt connected to your teammates, there was mutual respect, and a positive vibe was palpable throughout the team, right? You could feel the contagious enthusiasm in meetings and left energized and excited. That's "the Energy of Belonging!"

When the Energy Is Missing

"It's a depleting and diminishing feeling to go from an organization where I was truly part of a team to a place where no one would notice if I disappeared. I greatly miss the sense of belonging."

—Kade

While the presence of Belonging energizes or produces positive energy, the absence of it zaps energy from the team and actually produces negative energy. The results are staggering and detrimental to organizations: reduced creativity, decreased productivity, and lowered performance. "The Energy of Belonging" is generated or depleted with every human interaction.

In fact, BetterUp found that employees who felt excluded were 25% less productive.[15] Consider a team you were a part of where you didn't feel like you were a valued member. Maybe you were part of a team where no one:

- welcomed you into the team.
- expressed an interest in getting to know you.
- acknowledged or recognized your contributions, like that time you spent an entire weekend pulling together the annual report.
- stood up for you at a team meeting when someone interrupted you while you were speaking.

When we have experiences such as these, employees and the organization lack "the Energy of Belonging," which leads to the consequence of continuous energy drain.

The vitality of an organization is an essential building block for its success, and requires each employee to be infused with "the Energy of Belonging." Like dropping a pebble into a pond to create a positive, beautiful ripple effect, employees can give each other a spark to fuel "the Energy of Belonging." For, when employees feel *connected* to the people on their team, know their contributions and talents are *respected*, and trust the foundation of relationships among team members, so all feel *protected*, it is then when "the Energy of Belonging" becomes the precipitating factor in driving employee and organizational success.

First things first, how do we begin? In the next section, we are going to examine and learn about the key to sparking relationships; it starts when we all *connect*.

PART FOUR

CONNECT

Employees need to feel connected to their peers, leaders, and organizations.

Connected

to the people we work
with, our leaders, and
the organization

Respected

by the people we work
with and our leaders

Protected

by the promise that we
are safe to be and to
express ourself freely

WHY *CONNECTING* MATTERS

Brian's Story

"We go to the office on Tuesdays and Thursdays so we can socialize and do some work face-to-face. Every other week we bring our lunch and have it together; it's how we stay connected."

"Right after I was hired and before I started my new job, Melissa, my manager, sent me a personal welcome video. In it, she said, 'I want you to know how important you are, Brian. These are the skills you bring that we're really looking forward to leveraging (and she listed the skills). I can't wait for you to start.' In my first few weeks, I was tasked with reaching out to and getting to know the executives, upper-level managers, and leaders. I was amazed that so many of them already knew who I was, what skills I had, and how I was going to contribute to the company. They were so welcoming, and they continually showed their excitement for what I brought to the company and the work I was taking on. I couldn't believe the executives were excited about *me*!

"The same was true for my team members. They knew all about me when I started. They were eager to get to know me as a person and that really made me feel a part of the team on Day One. Now, even though there's not a requirement to be in the office on certain days, we all go in on Tuesdays and Thursdays so we can socialize and do some work face-to-face. Every other week, we bring our lunch and have it together. It's how we stay connected."

—Brian

Introduction

Brian's story clearly demonstrates how to *connect* at work and the positive impact that connection can have on employees. Brian was welcomed into his new work community and his new colleagues were interested in him before he even walked through the door on his first day. His manager, coworkers, and the senior executives made sure Brian felt connected to the organization. The simple practice of committing to eat lunch together regularly can sustain connection with all employees because it provides opportunities to be seen and heard as a human being, not just an employee.

The Meaning of *Connect*

Connection means something different to each of us. Here, it refers to employees really knowing their colleagues due to the time they spend together, which creates the bonds that nurture relationships. It includes the *shared* experiences that come from a *shared* purpose and contributing to *shared* goals and organizational success. These result in making employees feel cared for and motivating them to reciprocate, contributing to the sense of community. How important this sense of camaraderie is varies for each individual, but this need exists in all employees. For example, on an importance scale of one to ten, I would rate a sense of camaraderie a nine (very important); my husband would rate it a two (not so much).

WHAT DO YOU THINK?

How important is it for you to have a sense of community or camaraderie with your colleagues?

How do you or can you promote opportunities for *connection*?

When employees feel connected, they feel they are a part of their workplace community, part of a common experience. Environments where employees really know each other enjoy heightened engagement, energy, and morale. In fact, in their 2022 annual global culture study, O.C. Tanner found that people who feel more connected to their teams, leaders, and their organization have better work experiences, which include:

- producing great work output
- rapport with teammates
- above-average sense of well-being
- better coping mechanisms in stressful situations[16]

These better work experiences also produce better organizational results, such as increased productivity, more "promoters" on the Employer Net Promoter Score (eNPS) scale, and more employees who plan to stay with the company for at least six years (eNPS is a system to measure employee loyalty and satisfaction. "Promoters" are more loyal to the organization and have higher levels of satisfaction at work).[17] This was true before the COVID-19 pandemic and, since then, the need for connection has been magnified.

Defining *Connect*

Employees feel connected to their colleagues and leaders when:

- they feel seen and heard.
- their colleagues express genuine interest in them.
- their leaders listen attentively and prioritize time for one-on-one conversations.

Examples from Interviews and Belonging at Work Survey© Responses	
When employees are...	**They respond or feel...**
Seen and heard	"I feel connected to my colleagues when they say hello to me and ask how my client presentation went."
Shown genuine interest in as a person	"I like when we talk about our life outside of work and when they ask me about the photos on my desk."
Prioritized by their leader	"I feel connected to my leader when she honors our weekly one-on-one meeting even when she is super busy."

To *Connect* Is a Matter of Survival

We're biologically wired to be with others, to seek connection with other humans. Human connection responds to our universal, fundamental need to know that we are not alone. Our brains are wired to seek connection and avoid exclusion because, to a reptilian part of our brains, it's a matter of life and death. The amygdala is responsible for keeping us alive. It continually monitors our environment on the lookout for physical and emotional threats. It's a smart part of the brain, but it interprets every difficult situation as a threat to our survival. Exclusion is among those threats. The amygdala thinks: "If I'm alone, I will *die!*"

To survive, we must connect with other humans. At work, those "humans" are our colleagues and leaders. This connection results from being seen and heard as an individual and it creates a sense of belonging in a workplace community.

Connection Creates Community

A sense of connection to colleagues and leaders fosters a positive, motivated, and energized work environment. It enhances collaboration and teamwork because people know each other as humans, not just as employees. It fuels a sense of shared commitment to team goals because there is less "us and them" and more "we." Connection also fosters a sense of unity and shared vision. For example, at his university, Don coordinates an annual summer program that requires substantial collaboration between multiple departments. Seeing the students who come through the program eventually graduate from the school inspires a shared vision that motivates the employees throughout the school to go above and beyond to ensure the program is a success.

Connection comes down to caring. When others know us and are interested in us, we feel cared for as human beings. Many employees want their colleagues to know who they are, including tidbits* from the *Belonging at Work Survey*© like:

- what their favorite weekend hobbies are.
- that their son is competing in a soccer tournament next weekend.
- where they went on vacation.

*These tidbits will also vary for each individual. For example, my husband would not want his colleagues to know his favorite weekend hobby (playing video games), but he appreciates it when they bring him Snickers chocolate bars because they know he loves candy. The key to being "known" is when colleagues know each other well enough to know what makes each individual unique. The tidbits surface when employees take time to talk about non-work topics. In fact, the most common response to "I feel connected to my colleagues and leaders when…" is "talking with them about non-work stuff."

WOULD YOU DO THIS?

"When I took my dog to the vet, my coworker Fred sent me an IM the next day to ask how Scooby was doing. He doesn't even like dogs, but he knows how important Scooby is to me."

—*Belonging at Work Survey*© Response

The *Belonging at Work Survey*© results are similar in that they highlight how significant small actions are in becoming better acquainted with one's colleagues and peers.

Examples of Connection

"I couldn't hear much of what they were saying because of the clinking silverware, but they tried."

"Within my team, I felt very connected, even though I was the only one who worked remotely. One day back in 2012, my team took me out to lunch with them: once they were seated at the restaurant, one of my teammates called me on her cell phone and put the phone in the center of the table. I couldn't hear much of what they were saying because of the clinking silverware, and at one point the phone even fell off the table. But they tried! They made an effort to include me and that made all the difference."

—Chris

What I love about Chris' story is how much the effort meant to her even though the attempt to include her failed miserably. It shows how impactful it is to be intentional about seeing and hearing our colleagues. In today's hybrid work environments, being intentional about connecting is essential for employees who are not in the office.

Interviewees were remarkably straightforward when asked, "What's something that contributes to your sense of connection with the people with whom you work?" They consistently reinforced that it's not the big, magnanimous gestures, such as lavish off-site meetings or retreats, that create a sense of community. On the contrary, it's the tiny, simple interactions that create connection.

When I present to leaders in financial services about behaviors that strengthen connection at work, it's powerful to see their reactions to examples from their colleagues and direct reports. Participants in my programs complete my *Belonging at Work Survey*© before our first meeting as a group. The survey collects anonymous company-specific examples of connection. I use their language to reveal invaluable real-life insights about the culture, and it is one of the most impactful participant experiences in the program. For example, Kinecta Federal Credit Union has an internal newsletter called "The Kinection." One Kinecta team member shared on the survey that they feel connected to their colleagues when they read the "Tell Me Something Good" section and learn about their coworkers' lives outside of work. The impact of this single example of connection is amplified because it is specific to Kinecta and its employees.

While each organization has its unique experiences of belonging, there are universal examples across most organizations as to what a sense of connection is. Based on more than 1,500 responses to the *Belonging at Work Survey*©, listed below are ten of the most common ways employees feel connected to their colleagues and leaders.

Ten Common Ways to *Connect*

"I feel connected to my colleagues and leaders at work when..."

1. ...we talk about non-work topics like sports, movies, or vacations.
2. ...they say hello to me as I enter the conference room.
3. ...a smile leaps on their face when they see me.
4. ...they remember a fact about me or my family that I shared previously.
5. ...I am asked for my ideas, thoughts, and opinions.
6. ...they thank me for my contributions to a project or goal.
7. ...we share fun or funny moments together.
8. ...they send me an article or meme and say, "I thought of you when I saw this. Thought you might like it."
9. ...we work on a community service project together.
10. ...we celebrate together: birthdays, product launches, work anniversaries, etc.

Which of these examples resonate with you?

Belonging at Work Survey© Results

Connection to Leaders

Employees also need to feel a sense of connection to their leaders. They need to know that their managers know who they are as humans, that they want to know about their interests, care about their career goals, and know what's important to them. In short, employees need to know that their leaders care about them as individuals. The impact of feeling connected to leaders goes beyond belonging. In fact, in 2022, McKinsey's research on attrition found that not having caring leaders is one of the top three reasons employees leave a company.[18]

Employees and leaders don't have to be in the same office (or the same country!) to be connected. For example, when Marcey worked remotely as a clinical research associate, she felt very connected to her boss, Jackie, even though they worked together for six years before meeting in person. Jackie's genuine interest in Marcey strengthened their relationship. As Marcey shares, they knew each other as people: "Some people might not have felt strongly connected with their boss because they worked remotely, but I absolutely did. I think it was because we talked about our personal lives; like, I knew her, James, her husband, and Jay, her son. She'd ask about my husband Kevin's band. It wasn't just business." Jackie knew who Marcey was, even though they'd never met in person (and this was before the days of videoconferencing and webcams!).

Leaders: What Employees Wish You Knew about Connecting

The leaders of a healthcare organization I consulted with were eager for specific examples of how they can create and strengthen connections with their direct reports. The leaders' efforts to connect with employees fell short. Their internal employee engagement survey results indicated employees felt disconnected from their leaders.

The following prompt was included in a customized internal *Belonging at Work Survey*© that I prepared for their leadership and employees. It's important to ask questions that elicit organization-specific examples for connecting with others.

How would you complete this sentence?

"I wish my leaders knew I'd feel a stronger sense of connection if they…"

1.   …made an effort to get to know me as a person.
2.   …showed an interest in my input and ideas.
3.   …communicated with me more often.
4.   …asked me about my skills and experience.
5.   …shared the full plan or complete picture of where we are and where we're going, so we're all on the same page.

Which connections have you made at work recently?

Belonging at Work Survey© Results

The survey responses sparked an intense discussion amongst the leaders. They were shocked to read what their employees wanted. The survey responses helped them realize they had made assumptions about what they thought their employees wanted—wrong assumptions. As a result of this new perspective, we worked together as a group to develop new strategies for them to connect with their direct reports. The strategies were directly related to the survey responses. For example, David, one of the leaders, initiated walking meetings with his direct reports so they could get to know each other.

Connection to the Organization

> "When the new manager came in, I felt more connected with the organization's purpose and our mission. It was clear that everyone was working for good and for things that would improve the quality of life."
>
> —Johnna

Belonging at work comes from a connection to the organization, too. Employees feel connected to an organization when the company's values align with their own. Connection to the organization results when employees see how their work contributes to the organization's success. It also happens when employees can see that their personal values align with the organization's core values.

For example, I teach a course in leadership and management in high tech industries as part of Duke University's Engineering graduate programs. The program directors are committed to employing faculty with real experience in that area of study. I am not an engineer, but, for much of my corporate career, I was a training executive in high tech software companies.

When I accepted the faculty position at Duke, I worried, *will I belong in this community?* The answer was and is "yes," in part because the five core principles of the Engineering Management curriculum align with my personal values (Engineering Management is one of the graduate programs).

The Five Principles of Duke Engineering Management:

1. Communication
2. Teamwork
3. Critical Thinking
4. Ethics
5. Humanness[19]

My fellow faculty align with and embody these principles, which closely align with my values of compassion, collaboration, integrity, and empathy in the workplace and beyond. I feel connected to Duke University's Pratt School of Engineering because my personal values align with the school's values.

By the way, intentionally including others in your work, such as in team projects or asking a colleague for their advice, contributes to a sense of connection to the organization.[20] Connecting with colleagues does double duty by fostering connection to peers *and* to the organization![21]

When *Connection* Is Missing

When employees don't feel connected to the people they work with, they often feel excluded or invisible. Sadly, disconnection is prevalent in today's workplaces: 65% of employees say they feel less connected to their coworkers.[22] With today's work environments shifting between remote, hybrid, and return to office arrangements, I have no doubt this percentage is even higher. According to Gallup's 2022 State of the Workplace Report, only 20% of employees say they have a best friend at work.

Disconnection is costly in multiple ways, including:

- higher risk of turnover (up to 50% higher)[23]
- lower work quality
- reduced productivity (up to 25% less)[24]
- reduced willingness to contribute to team goals
- more missed workdays[25]

Take Kade's story, for example. How productive do you think he is? Is he likely to go all out to help with next month's product launch? Probably not.

"I don't feel like I'm a part of this team."

"In this new job, my coworkers are all very connected to one another. They are very much a group: they go to dinner, hang out after work, and go to ball games together. I hear them chitchatting in one of their offices. But very few people have deliberately come to talk to me. The guy next to me won't even look at me, and he's gay, too! I work from home more than I intended to because I don't enjoy that workspace. I don't like feeling that I don't belong or like I'm driving somewhere to simply occupy a chair instead of being a part of a community. I'm usually a team player, willing to do whatever it takes to help my coworkers. But I don't feel like I'm a part of this team. As a result, I am not engaged in the work I'm doing. It's affecting my quality of work and my commitment to it.

—Kade

How connected do you think Chris and other remote employees felt with those at the headquarter office?

"Everything they did was headquarter-centric."

"As a virtual employee, I never felt like I had a voice or that anybody cared about employees who weren't based at headquarters. Even though we had locations across the country, all the events were held at the home office. They spent tons of money on fun, elaborate all-hands meetings with beach balls and live music, but only in that one location.

"Meetings were always scheduled based on their time zone. They'd forget to include a Zoom link in meeting invitations. They had side conversations in the hallways and never looped in the people in the Detroit office who needed to know the plans had changed. Everything they did was headquarter-centric, and they made no effort to think about anyone who wasn't located there. They never thought about the experience we had as employees who worked from home or in one of the other offices. I always felt close to my teammates, but never felt connected to the organization because I felt like they didn't care about me."

—Chris

Many organizations use contractors or freelancers to do essential work. Are they included like other employees, or are they excluded like Marcey?

"I felt so isolated and excluded."

"I got my first real job when I was in graduate school. I was a government contractor running the wellness program and fitness center at a federal health-related agency. In December, they had a holiday party, and I was the only person who was not invited. They said it was because I was a contractor, and the party was for 'employees.' It felt like a class system. I felt so isolated and excluded."

—Marcey

---

25 Simple Ideas to Spark *Connection* at Work

Employees feel connected to others when they feel seen and heard, when others show interest in them as people. Results from over 1,500 survey responses indicate that employees feel connected to the people they work with when they talk about non-work topics and spend time getting to know each other as human beings.

What can employees do to foster connections with their peers and leaders? Below are 25 ideas to see, hear, and learn more about the people in your workplace community. My hope is that you will see how simple these ideas are and that they will inspire you to come up with new ones. They may not all work for your organization, but I am confident many of them will. Get creative: experiment with modifying them to add your own spark. Have fun connecting!

Invite Individual Conversations

Show your coworkers you are interested in getting to know them by inviting them into a conversation.

1. Invite someone to join you for a short break.

Invite someone you don't know well to join you for a "movement break" such as a walk, a workout, or a mental break. Getting to know your colleagues one-on-one by spending time with them away from your desks shows you are interested in learning more about them as individuals.

Keep it simple and walk around your office building, or even off-site, depending on your work setting. Challenge yourself to "meet" five colleagues in your office within the next thirty days. It's extra nice when you invite someone who is new to the organization, or someone you don't yet know. This is also fun to do as a group (described in Idea #17).

2. Check on a colleague who is experiencing a challenge.

When you become aware of a colleague facing a challenge, a few kind words of compassion can go a long way to show you care about them. The challenge could be anything from a difficult customer meeting to severe weather to a parent's illness. It's okay if you don't know the details of their situation. Show your colleagues you care about them by sending them a text or voicemail to check on them. It lets them know you are thinking about them. Even if they don't receive the message immediately, just reaching out shows you care.

If there is something you can do to help them, such as offering to lead an upcoming meeting or rescheduling a project deadline, then make the offer. Please don't say, "If I can do anything to help, just let me know!" This statement puts the burden on them to ask for help.

3. Invite a colleague to join your conversation.

Isn't it awkward to walk into a meeting room, conference room, or virtual meeting where groups of people are already deeply engaged in conversation? Many people are uncomfortable joining a group in the middle of a conversation. Making the effort to prevent another person from feeling awkward conveys that you see and care about them.

Alleviate the awkwardness by proactively asking someone who is alone if you can join them or inviting a person who enters the room to join your conversation.

4. Invite someone who enters the room to sit next to you.

It can be awkward to enter a conference or dining room and not know where to sit. Like joining conversations in progress, many people feel uneasy about choosing a seat. Making the effort to prevent someone from feeling that way shows you see them and are interested in making them feel welcome.

Invite a colleague or leader you don't know well who comes into the room to sit at your table. They will appreciate the invitation.

5. Explain inside jokes or funny shared memories to new team members.

When some employees reminisce about a shared memory, the employees who were not there may feel excluded or left out. It's great to remember fun times, and the communal laughter can be a welcome relief. During those moments of shared laughter, make an effort to take a few moments to bring everyone into the situation and explain the joke or memory to anyone who wasn't there when it happened. Ask others to share their own funny shared memories or similar situations.

Invigorate Others

Show your colleagues you are thinking about them to strengthen your relationships and energize them.

6. Make a personal commitment to say "thank you" to someone every week.

Challenge yourself to say thank you to a colleague or leader at least once a week (feel free to adjust the number or frequency). A simple "thank you" is an easy yet impactful way to connect with others because it demonstrates you see them and what they do.

Send them an email, call them, or better yet, express your gratitude in person whenever you can. Be specific about what you're thanking them for and the impact it had.

7. Send a coworker a silly emoji text or instant message just saying "hello."

Without a single word, you can say, "Hello. I'm thinking of you." It doesn't have to be a magnanimous gesture to connect with a colleague. Just letting them know you are thinking about them can brighten their day.

For example, one of my clients sends wordless text messages and instant messages to her colleagues. She delights in finding an obscure or random emoji or gif to elicit a smile from the recipient.

8. Post a "shout-out" about a colleague on internal social media or in your company newsletter.*

Let your organization know how grateful you are for a colleague's help on your project with a "shout-out" on internal communication channels. Recognition goes a long way in building connection because it acknowledges an individual's work.

*Be careful: some of your coworkers may not want *public* recognition. Respect their preference for staying out of the limelight and send them a private "shout-out" instead to express your gratitude.

9. Acknowledge a colleague's religious, holiday, or cultural celebrations.

Demonstrate interest in your colleagues by recognizing, acknowledging, and/or asking about an upcoming holiday or cultural celebration that is important to them. Your interest conveys a desire to get to know them as an individual and strengthens rapport.

For example, Diwali, also known as the Festival of Lights, is an important autumn festival in some Indian religions. If you have a coworker from India who mentions Diwali, you could ask them if they celebrate Diwali, as well as inquire about their favorite part of the festival.

10. Offer to help a colleague.

Think about who in your group is deep in a project right now. What might you offer to do to help them? It doesn't have to be a big offer to be meaningful and deepen the connection between you. If you're unsure about how to best help a colleague, make a specific offer and add that you'd be happy to assist in a different way if they have other ideas for taking you up on your offer.

For example, think about a time when you were neck-deep in a project and were fretting that it was your turn to facilitate the team meeting. Remember how relieved you were when Don offered to switch dates with you so you could focus on your project?

Integrate Connection Activities into Team Meetings

Build in time to deepen relationships when you are together.

11. Start meetings with a brief check-in to see how everyone is doing.

Take a few minutes at the beginning of meetings to invite attendees to describe how they are doing. Acknowledging everyone's current state of mind builds rapport and helps your team become fully present.

Worried about how long this process will take? Employ this efficient "Two Words" strategy from author Brené Brown, who uses it to ensure this essential part of her team meetings stays brief: each person shares two words that describe how they are feeling that day.[26] There are no explanations or elaboration, just genuine connection.

12. Add two to three minutes to your team meetings occasionally for "shout-outs" and "kudos."

Every now and then, include in your team meeting agendas a few minutes for employees to recognize their coworkers' recent contributions and achievements. Acknowledging and appreciating others' successes builds rapport and deepens relationships within your team.

The team can use this time to recognize a colleague's help on a project or express gratitude for others remembering their work anniversary.

13. Spend five minutes at the beginning of a meeting sharing something funny.

At the beginning of your next team meeting, spend five minutes sharing a fun or funny experience. Considering we spend so much work time in meetings, they can provide optimal opportunities to deepen connections among colleagues.

For example, you might invite everyone (or a few people) to share:

- one of the last ten photos on their phone and explain it
- a funny story or memory related to an upcoming holiday
- the funniest autocorrect mistakes they've seen
- a funny memory from grade school or a summer vacation

14. Add "lightning rounds" to meetings or gatherings.

Set aside a few minutes on an upcoming team meeting agenda to get to know each other with a lightning round with three to five questions. Lightning rounds are a series of rapid-fire questions that have short answers. They provide an opportunity for you to learn more about the people on your team in a short period of time.

For example, in one of my classes I asked these five questions and randomly called on students to respond:

What is:

- your favorite day of the week?
- one thing that makes you laugh out loud?
- your favorite snack?
- one country you want to visit?
- your seat preference on a plane: window or aisle seat?

15. Create an opportunity in a group meeting for colleagues to share something about their culture or heritage.

Dedicate a few minutes during your next team/project meeting, lunch break, or movement break to invite team members to share something about their culture or heritage. Learning more about your colleagues' culture or heritage (and them learning about yours) provides an opportunity to deepen your relationship.

Choose a theme such as:

- An upcoming holiday, such as Independence Day or New Year's: "What does 'independence' mean to you?"
- Birthday celebration traditions
- Describe a color that has a special meaning in your culture
- Share a rite of passage tradition in your culture or family
- Describe a food that is especially meaningful in your culture, heritage, or family

Initiate Events Beyond Your Team

Expand your efforts by creating shared experiences with colleagues and leaders outside your immediate team.

16. Commit to eating lunch together away from your desks.

Whether you're working in the office or from home, set a lunchtime meeting periodically for anyone interested in eating together and commit to discussing only non-work-related topics. The informal gathering provides an opportunity to get to know others as individuals.

For example, "on the first Thursday of the month at 12:30 PM, meet in the break room for lunch." If you and your colleagues work remotely, open a virtual meeting for conversations during the lunch break. Accommodate multiple time zones by turning the event into a break instead of lunch. The key idea is to disconnect from your work and connect with your colleagues.

17. Go on a fifteen-minute walk as a group.

Get away from your desk and get moving by setting a regular break time for a fifteen-minute walk. Similar to eating lunch together, schedule a recurring regular (or even an occasional) walking break, such as from 10:00 to 10:15 AM. Taking brief movement breaks throughout the day increases your productivity and focus. Optimize break time by using it to connect with your colleagues. This idea can work for a small group of people in the same physical location and those working remotely. If the weather is bad, walk around inside the office for fifteen minutes. Use a conference call for a virtual group walk.

For example, my friend Marcey and I occasionally go on what she calls "walkie-talkies." We walk in our respective neighborhoods while we talk on our phones. The break is helpful for our brains, our bodies, and our connection to each other.

18. Host a book club or a video club.

Start a book or video club that meets regularly to discuss insights from the selected book or video. Informal clubs encourage coworkers to get together and develop deeper relationships through shared experiences. For a video club, you can rotate responsibility for selecting a TEDx Talk or other short video to view and facilitate a discussion, perhaps as you eat breakfast or lunch together. For a book club, you could rotate the responsibility for coordinating the next club meeting. This is a great opportunity to get to know people in other departments or teams.

19. Host a cooking class virtually or in person.

Enlist the expertise of a local chef to host a cooking demonstration online or at a local restaurant during off hours for a cooking lesson. This is a great time to create new memories and shared experiences that are not work-related. The chef can call on participants to chop vegetables, measure spices, or stir the sauce as it cooks.

Adaptation: you can also host a virtual cooking class yourself. Share a simple recipe with others and schedule the class. Before the class, everyone gathers the necessary ingredients, equipment, and the recipe. During the virtual class, demonstrate how to prepare the recipe and, after everyone has prepared it, you can enjoy the dish together when it's ready.

20. Coordinate a community service event.

Create an opportunity for coworkers to spend time together volunteering or giving back to your community. Experiencing a non-work-related event with others creates meaningful shared memories that strengthen the connection among colleagues. The event doesn't have to be huge or deeply structured. It can be as simple as a one- to two-hour event picking up trash at a nearby community park. Remote employees can also participate by performing the same or a similar service in their local communities.

Incorporate Play and Self-Care

Create time with your colleagues and leaders for laughter, fun, and well-being.

21. Create a team playlist of go-to songs.

Ask your colleagues to share one of their favorite energizing songs— one that lifts them up or makes them happy. Create and share a playlist of everyone's go-to songs and play it as people gather for meetings or events. The playlist provides an interesting peek inside others' musical tastes and an opportunity to learn more about your coworkers.

For example, I teach at 8:30 on Monday mornings. At the beginning of each semester, each of my students sends me one of their Monday morning go-to songs. I create a playlist and play it as they come into class and during breaks. It's entertaining to see them sing and dance and get excited when they hear their go-to-song or another song they like.

22. Host a "Show and Tell Showcase."

Host an occasional ten- or fifteen-minute break where a few employees bring an object, photo, or book that they are proud of or has a special meaning for them. The event provides time and space to get to know each other more deeply as employees take turns explaining what it is, the story behind it, and why it is meaningful to them.

Schedule a fifteen-minute "Show and Tell Showcase" meeting in the next month and invite a few colleagues. Model how it works by bringing an object that is important to you. Explain what it is and how its meaning made itself known to you. Announce the next "Show and Tell Showcase" meeting date and ask for two or three volunteers to share an object, photo, or book of their choice.

23. Play a "Get to Know You" game.

Initiate opportunities for employees to get to know each other with an occasional ten- or fifteen-minute game break. Games take little time to prepare and offer a fun chance to let off steam and learn more about your colleagues.

For example, in "Two Truths and a Lie," several employees share two truths and a lie about themselves. The truths and the lies often generate spirited conversations where everyone gets to know each other better as they laugh at the creative truths and lies.

24. Share your passion projects.

Host occasional before- or after-hours meetings or breaks where one or two employees spend ten or fifteen minutes sharing something they're passionate about. Shining light on what matters to us is an investment in our self-care. Passion projects connect you to what matters to others (and you) and show your colleagues you are interested in them as human beings (and they are interested in you!).

You just might discover some of your colleagues are avid beekeepers or acoustic guitar players, or are learning to make a kite.

25. Share self-care or well-being strategies.

You can never have too many strategies for taking care of yourself. Many of us have a selection of go-to self-care practices. Share one or two of them with your colleagues! This short activity promotes self-care and provides time for you and your coworkers to learn about each other. At the beginning or end of a team meeting, invite a few team members to share one of their favorite well-being practices and why they find it helpful.

Download all 25 ideas to spark
connections:
www.BelongingEnergy.com

Outcomes When We *Connect*

Employee disconnection is one of the main contributors to voluntary turnover in organizations. It doesn't have to be that way. Employees thrive and grow when they have a strong sense of connection to their colleagues, leaders, and the organization. The Institute of Leadership and Management reported in 2020 that 77% of respondents said that building close relationships at work is the most important factor in determining their job satisfaction. Surprisingly, salary was eighth on the list![27] Employees who have meaningful, purposeful relationships at work:

- Produce higher quality work
- Have fewer on the job injuries
- Report higher well-being

Luis's experience described below demonstrates the positive and motivating impact a caring leader can have:

"Ana was the best boss I ever had."

"Ana was the best boss I ever had. Even though she was busy, she always made me feel like I was the most important thing to her when we talked because she had this ability to give you her undivided attention. I never had the feeling that she had other things to do. It was clear that she wasn't just looking for bodies to get work done. She cared about me as a person. She was one of those mentors who would tell you what you don't want to hear in a way that made it clear she had your back. She would say, 'Luis, you didn't show up on this project' or 'You need to do better with your presenting.' I knew without a doubt that she gave me the feedback I needed to grow."

—Luis

Reflection

When we reflect on what we are learning and apply it to our own lives, our learning deepens, and we are more likely to act on what we learn. These questions invite you to reflect on your own experiences with connection at work.

1. What's one thing someone at work did to you or for you recently that made you feel welcome or included?

2. Think back to a situation or experience in your work life when you felt disconnected or excluded from, or ignored by, your colleagues and/or your leader. Describe the situation. What made this experience memorable for you?

3. What thoughts did you think and what did you feel when it happened?

4. What lessons did you learn from this experience? How have they impacted who you are today?

5. Consider the people you work with: who might be feeling disconnected right now? Choose one of the *connect* ideas to reconnect with them. Which spark will you use?

From *Connect* to *Respect*

At the beginning of the chapter, Brian was amazed that his new colleagues and the senior leaders in his company knew who he was, knew the skills he brought to the company, and were excited to meet him. He felt *connected* to his colleagues, leaders, and to the organization from Day One.

We're biologically wired to *connect* with other people. To feel a sense of belonging at work, employees need to feel connected to the people they work with and to the organization. When this innate human need is met, employees are more productive, more engaged, more innovative, and less likely to leave. Employees are connected when they are seen and heard by their peers and leaders, when the people in their work community really know each other as people. Simple behaviors like saying "hello" when someone walks into the conference room create connection.

To further *connect* with our organization, in our next section, we explore how *respect* contributes to Belonging at work.

PART FIVE

RESPECT

Employees need to know that their time, talent, and contributions matter.

Connected

to the people we work
with, our leaders, and
the organization

Respected

by the people we work
with and our leaders

Protected

by the promise that we
are safe to be and to
express ourself freely

WHY RESPECT MATTERS

Michael's Story

"It meant a lot to me to give and receive the silly high fives."

"We celebrate 'Team Member Appreciation Week,' which is half-way through our fiscal year. We recognize our team members in different ways throughout the week. Last year, during our weekly managers' meeting, one of my managers had us do a high five activity. We traced our hands on paper and made hand cutouts. Throughout the week, employees wrote a team member's name on a cutout and what they did to warrant a high five. We posted the high fives on a bulletin board in our area. By the end of the week, the bulletin board was totally filled with high fives. It was silly, but it was also fun, too. It was so cool to know that a team member really appreciated something I did that I thought was small or insignificant. It meant a lot to me to give and receive the silly high fives."

—Michael

Introduction

Michael's Team Member Appreciation Week experience illustrates the impact that recognition can have on an employee's spirit. It also shows how simple (and fun!) it can be to say, "I see and appreciate what you do."

The Meaning of *Respect*

The relationship between feeling respected and a sense of belonging is a powerful cycle: when employees know they are valued and appreciated, they believe that what they do matters to others and to the organization. That belief, when energized by recognition and acknowledgement, deepens their sense of belonging, which, in turn, fuels their commitment to and engagement in their workplace community. Employees want to be recognized for their talents and contributions. They need to know that they are respected and valued by their peers and leaders. They crave acknowledgement from others, for others to see how their unique skills make a difference in the organization.

HOW WOULD THIS MAKE YOU FEEL?

"My boss said, 'I can finally get some things accomplished that I've wanted to do because I have someone with the skill set we need to do them.'"

—Johnna

Who can you acknowledge today?

In 2020, Coqual, the global think tank and advisory group, published the results of their fascinating research on Belonging at work. Not surprisingly, they found *respect* is a huge contributor to belonging in supportive peer workplace communities.[28] I was not surprised they found that peer praise and appreciation impact employees' sense of Belonging, as does honest, open communication about work relationships. What I was surprised to see was how important our colleagues' respect *for outside commitments* such as caregiving or carpool duty was as a contributor to our sense of belonging. When I reflected on why this insight surprised me, I realized that this makes perfect sense: **respect for non-work commitments is related to *connection*.** Many employees want their colleagues to know about and *respect* their life outside of work. This finding speaks to our desire to be seen as and respected for being whole humans with lives separate from work.

Similar to *connect*, *respect* is unique to each individual. What is common is that employees feel respected when they are given:

- opportunities to provide input on decisions
- trust and autonomy to decide how they do their work
- support from peers and leaders for their decisions
- recognition for their contributions
- timely responses to emails

Examples from Interviews and Survey Responses	
When employees are...	**They respond or feel...**
Invited to provide input or feedback about decisions or projects	"I feel respected at work when my opinion is discussed, even if we decide to go another way."
Trusted to make decisions	"I feel respected when I am not micromanaged and can do work my way."
Recognized and appreciated for their skills and talents	"I feel respected by my leaders when they acknowledge my accomplishments."

As a new Duke faculty member, I was invited to be one of the presenters at student orientation for the Engineering Management graduate program. The orientation session was organized around the following principles, mentioned earlier:

Five Duke Engineering Management Principles

- Communication
- Teamwork
- Critical Thinking
- Ethics
- Humanness

Because of my Belonging work, I was asked to speak about "Humanness." I was elated and moved to be invited! The invitation to be part of the orientation team conveyed to me that my colleagues recognized my knowledge and experience; the team valued my skills and thought they would be valuable to students. It was a meaningful message to me that I was a respected member of the community.

Interviewees consistently reiterated the essential role respect plays in fostering a culture of Belonging at work. They shared examples of how included they felt when they were:

- recognized for their talents
- invited to be involved in discussions
- received (or given) autonomy in their work

Being respected increased their job satisfaction, their productivity, and their commitment to their coworkers and to the company.

They also shared the hurt that comes when they don't feel respected.

HOW WOULD THIS MAKE YOU FEEL?

"People would walk around the office right at five o'clock to see who was still there. They made value judgments about the people who stayed after five o'clock, how hard they worked, their work ethic and the value they provided the organization. Anyone who didn't stay late was lazy or not committed to the organization."

—Elizabeth

Is there a behavior you are doing that could be changed to show more respect to your coworkers?

When *Respect* Is Missing

When employees don't feel respected, the negative consequences can range from them withholding their creative ideas, essential knowledge, and potential solutions instead of contributing to a project's success to reduced productivity, "quiet quitting," and engaging in "presenteeism" (showing up to work, but not doing any). The organization misses out on the employees' unique perspectives and ideas and the sense of community is diluted. In fact, in their 2022 Workplace Learning Report, researchers at LinkedIn reported that employees who feel their skills are not being put to good use are ten times more likely to look for a new job.[29]

Samantha's story below demonstrates the impact a lack of respect can have even when you are not the one being targeted.

"Our new CEO came in and started cursing on conference calls and disparaging some of the leaders."

"I'd been working at this company for eleven years. I loved the direction we were taking related to fundamental leadership, communication skills, and behaviors that drove the culture I thought we were working towards. But then, our new CEO came in and started cursing on conference calls and disparaging others, particularly many of the leaders. Some of these leaders were non-degreed at the time, had worked for numerous years for the organization, and had built successful divisions without having a degree. The new CEO ridiculed their lack of education. He made assumptions and negative comments about them.

"He literally referred to people as 'fucking asshole managers who needed to get their heads out of their asses.' Looking back, I think he was taking a Bobby Knight approach, trying to spur motivation by yelling at them. But putting people down doesn't get them to rally. While this didn't affect me directly, I felt its effects on other people.

Ultimately, I left the organization after working there for eleven years because it was incongruent with my belief system. The work I was doing in leadership, communication, and culture was ultimately not being modeled at the top level. Any kind of change in behavior we inspired in middle management was not going to be sustainable if the top leadership acted differently."

—Samantha

Examples of *Respect*

When I present to education leaders about the role respect plays in fostering Belonging in their work world, the examples they share in the *Belonging at Work Survey*© are powerful. Reminder: The survey collects anonymous audience-specific examples of respect, using their language to reveal invaluable real-life insights about their community's culture. For example, Delta Kappa Gamma (DKG) is an international society for key women educators. One DKG member explained in the survey that she feels respected when her colleagues ask for her perspective about a situation because of her specific skills and experience working with parents of children with disabilities.

Far from magnanimous, billboard-sized gestures, my research found it's simple, ordinary actions that contribute to people feeling respected and valued at work.

While each organization has its unique instances of experiences of Belonging, there are common examples of what respecting individuals looks like. The following examples represent several of the themes that emerged from the research interviews and survey results.

Ten Common Ways to *Respect*

"I feel respected by my colleagues and leaders at work when..."

1. ...they acknowledge my work in a positive way.
2. ...they invite me to provide input on ideas and goals.
3. ...they trust me to make decisions.
4. ...I am included in meetings and have a voice in decisions.
5. ...we openly discuss ideas, perspectives, and opinions.
6. ...they show interest in my career development.
7. ...my decisions and ideas are supported, even if they're counter to the norm.
8. ...everyone on my team is supported equally, regardless of position.
9. ...they give me feedback in a constructive, supportive way.
10. ...they rely on me to complete an important task.

Which of these sound familiar to you?

Belonging at Work Survey© Results

What Your Colleagues and Employees Wish You Know about *Respect*

We tend to overcomplicate the behaviors that we think demonstrate respect. Your colleagues wish you knew just how much the small things you do mean to them. From more than 1,500 *Belonging at Work Survey©* responses, one of the most common ways to show respect is the simplest (and quickest): "I feel respected by my colleagues when they thank me for my contributions."

When I worked with engineering professionals in one organization, they asked for specific examples of ways to help their colleagues feel more respected at work. When I prepare for my keynote presentations and programs, collecting examples from within the organization is an essential component of my consulting work because it brings relevant examples from *their* world, *their* people, and in *their* language to the forefront.

The following prompt was included in an internal *Belonging at Work Survey©* I prepared to do some consulting and speaking for this company's leadership and employees. Common responses from their colleagues are below the prompt. How would you complete the sentence?

"I wish my leaders and team members knew I'd feel more respected by them if they…"

- …learned how to spell my name.
- …respected my time away from work.
- …walked the walk (like not sending emails after 6 PM).
- …didn't blindside our group with decisions they knew were coming.
- …invited me to provide input about a project.

How would you complete the sentence?

The engineers were stunned by the simple behaviors their colleagues said conveyed respect. It's not rocket science! Seeing their colleagues' survey responses on the PowerPoint slide was eye-opening for the engineers. We discussed the idea that sometimes hearing directly (even if anonymously) from a coworker or a direct report reminds us how important it is to acknowledge, recognize, appreciate, and listen. Building a culture of Belonging in your workplace community does not have to be complicated.

> "One of our biggest leadership problems right now is emotional illiteracy and a lack of understanding of what people need in order to feel appreciated."
>
> —Don

25 Simple Ideas to Show *Respect* at Work

Employees feel respected when their contributions and talents are acknowledged, when they have input into decisions and autonomy over how they do their work. Results from over 1,500 survey responses indicate that employees feel respected when their work is appreciated.

What can employees do to show colleagues, team members, and direct reports the respect they deserve and crave? Below are twenty-five ideas for ways to demonstrate respect for the time, talents, and contributions others make in your workplace community. My hope is that you will see how simple these ideas are and that they inspire you. While they may not all work for your organization, I am confident many of them will. Adapt them to use with peers, team members, and colleagues in other departments or groups. They can be used in person and virtually. Get creative: experiment with modifying them to add your own spark!

Engage Fully with Others

Show your colleagues you respect them by being fully present with them and acknowledging their brilliance.

1. Give them your undivided attention.

Give the colleague you're speaking with your *undivided* and *undistracted* attention. During meetings and conversations, close your email application and browsers. Note: closing browsers is different from minimizing them, as there is a cognitive difference between the two actions. Minimizing a browser or your inbox maintains a hold on your attention, but when you close them, you free up that mental energy. Plus, closing browsers and distracting applications make a stronger cognitive commitment to remove them as distractions. The act conveys to your brain and the other person that they deserve your full focus.

The same philosophy applies to your phone: put your cell phone *away,* as in literally out of sight, instead of face down on your desk during a conversation. When your phone is in your line of sight, it consumes some of your attention. (We see you glancing at it, even though you think you're being slick! No judgment here. I'm guilty of the same behavior.) Enable the "Do Not Disturb" function so you are not distracted by notification buzzes.

2. Listen attentively to your colleagues with the intention of understanding them fully.

While your coworker is speaking, make eye contact and nod or shake your head to indicate that you hear what they are saying. Giving someone your attention, demonstrating you are listening, and seeking to understand their perspective show that you value them as a person.

Ask a thoughtful question that shows you want to understand their perspective. Below are five questions you can use to seek to understand another person's perspective.

Choose one or two to ask in your next conversation.

- "What led you to choose X?"
- "What was that like for you?"
- "Can you tell me more?"
- "What sense have you been able to make of it so far?"
- "Are those the outcomes you expected?"

3. Provide positive feedback to a colleague for their impactful contributions.

Give a coworker specific, detailed positive feedback about their talents and/or contributions to a recent project's success. One of the easiest and often overlooked ways to show someone that you value their talents and contributions is simply to let them know you see and appreciate those talents and their impact. Be specific when you express your appreciation.

For example, you might say, "Denise, thank you for preparing the data for the client meeting. I appreciate the way you organized it, especially because you made it so easy to insert into the slide deck."

4. Highlight a colleague's strengths when speaking to them and others.

Help others see their amazingness. Drawing their attention to their own capabilities demonstrates you see something in them they may take for granted. In one-on-one conversations or in team meetings, acknowledge and recognize the specific skills and talents you appreciate in your coworkers. For example, "Joe, I admire the way you concisely summarize the key outcomes of our meetings." This small gesture tells Joe that you see and appreciate his talent.

5. Tell others when you learn something from them.

We learn new things from other people every day. When someone teaches you something, let them know what you've learned from them. Whether it's something big, like Sandy showing us how to format a report using the new corporate template, or something small, like Todd teaching us about a time-saving trick for peeling apples, they will feel good knowing they have taught you something helpful. It shows them you respect and appreciate their knowledge.

You can say something as simple as, "Todd, I used your apple-peeling hack this weekend and it saved me so much time. Thank you!"

Ensure People Are Seen and Honored

Be intentional about seeing others as they want to be seen.

6. Learn to pronounce their name correctly.

People with uncommon or hard to pronounce names are used to having their names mispronounced. Show them respect by making the effort to learn to pronounce their name correctly. You may stumble a few times, but your commitment conveys you honor who they are and will be worth it.

Invest a few moments and be vulnerable enough to ask for their help in learning to say it right, even if you must ask them more than once. Write it phonetically and practice it out loud.

7. Use their gender pronouns.

For many people, gender pronouns are not particularly significant. However, for others, pronouns hold specific and deep meaning. If you work with someone for whom gender pronouns are important, try to use them. Even if you don't always remember, your concerted effort demonstrates that you respect their gender identity. Ask them for and make an effort to use their gender pronouns.

8. **Use diverse images in presentations and other materials.**

While designing presentations and other materials, be intentional in using images that reflect your colleagues in terms of their visible characteristics, such as ethnicity, physical ability, gender, age, and culture. Taking the time to ensure the diversity of your team is reflected in your visual materials conveys your commitment to making sure your colleagues are honored.

While not every visible characteristic needs to be reflected in every presentation or document, try to use images that reflect the people with whom you work.

9. **Discuss work or career goals and interests. Look for opportunities to support them.**

Even if you are not a supervisor or leader, you and your colleagues can support each other's career goals and aspirations. Conversations about professional interests foster connection because you get to know each other better. It also builds mutual respect for your professional paths and can foster growth.

For example, you can recommend Derrick to the onboarding program project lead if you know he is interested in becoming more involved in the new hire experience.

10. **Honor your colleagues' time by being intentional about meetings.**

Time is a finite resource and one of our most closely guarded, prized possessions. Be intentional, thoughtful, and respectful of others' time when you make a demand on it.

When scheduling a meeting, consider whether it is really needed. Could it be an email or a quick phone conversation instead? If a meeting is truly needed, consider how long it needs to be (does it really need to be thirty or sixty minutes?). Sometimes a fifteen-minute meeting or phone call is sufficient. Also, honor their time by committing to start and end meetings on time.

Ensure All Voices Are Heard

Honor your coworkers by making sure their voices are heard respectfully.

11. Invite your colleague who has relevant experience or knowledge to a project meeting to contribute their insights.

Show respect for your coworker's previous experience by inviting them to a meeting where their insights will be helpful. They will feel included, connected, and that their prior experience brings value to others.

For example, during the planning team meeting for the customer service application rollout, you remember that Francisco spearheaded the implementation of a customer service application at his former employer. Ask the project organizer if it's okay to invite Francisco to the next planning meeting to share any lessons and best practices relevant to the project that he's learned.

12. Ensure everyone has a chance to speak and provide their input during meetings.

During group or team meetings, ensure that all participants are given the opportunity to contribute their input. It is common for certain colleagues to share their opinions and provide their input before others have had a chance. Those who naturally wait until there's an opening in the discussion or until they're asked sometimes don't get heard. Respectfully and diplomatically ensure all voices are heard and that everyone is invited to share their voice in ways that honor them.

This could mean saying to Melinda, who's already voiced her input, something like, "Melinda, hold on to your thought. Let's give Meijing and Keith a chance to say what they think. Keith or Meijing, would you like to add to what's been said already?"

13. Don't allow someone to interrupt someone else who is speaking.

Interrupting a person who is speaking is disrespectful and communicates, "what I have to say is more important than what you are saying."

When this behavior is left unchecked, the message sent to everyone present is that the behavior is acceptable. It reinforces an unhealthy dynamic that lacks respect and courtesy. Establish a team expectation that they should not interrupt those speaking.

Diplomatically address interrupters in a way that conveys respect for the person who was speaking, even if you're not the official leader in the situation.

14. Point out a viable piece of a coworker's recommendation or opinion.

When a person's ideas are dismissed or discounted by others, they can feel disrespected. Adopt a proactive approach to counter this feeling by pointing out the merits of a colleague's idea or suggestion. You don't have to agree with 100% of it to support them. You can highlight a specific part of it.

For example, you might say something like, "What I really like about Freda's idea is how it highlights our Q1 achievement..." or "I like Benjamin's framework because it addresses specifically what the client requested in our last meeting."

15. Disagree diplomatically without making the other person "wrong."

Diversity of perspectives enriches creativity and generates more powerful solutions. The bigger the group, the more likely it is there will be differences of opinions and perspectives. How you handle disagreements provides an opportunity to convey respect for all opinions.

Since we usually think our way is the "right" or "best" one, our language may communicate that others' ideas are wrong. Use the sample phrases below as you communicate your opinion to respectfully acknowledge the difference of perspective:

- "I had a different experience..."
- "I see that situation differently..."
- "What I drew from that conversation was..."

Enlist Input and Expertise

Show your colleagues you value their knowledge and experience by inviting them to share it.

16. Ask for others' opinions on and input in decisions.

Provide opportunities for team members to voice their thoughts and opinions about team decisions or priorities. Employees feel respected when they can have input into decisions. *Note: having a voice in decisions does not mean you are committing to go with their ideas; it means you are genuinely open to hearing and considering them.

Questions like the ones below can be used during meetings and one-on-one conversations to elicit input.

- "What ideas and recommendations do you have for the Acme project?"
- "There are a few paths we could take on Project Z. What do you think we should consider as we decide on the path?"
- "What are your thoughts about how we should prioritize these three projects?"

17. Ask a colleague to explain (not "defend") their thought process about a decision, project, or approach.

A group of people with diverse opinions and thought processes is a strength, and it provides a perfect opportunity to learn to think differently. Learning how others approach the decision-making, planning, or implementation process can help everyone on the team develop a broader set of analysis and critical thinking tools, and it demonstrates appreciation for your differences.

Ask a colleague who tackles projects differently to explain their thought process. Be sure to ask with a mindset of wanting to understand them, not to critique their methodology. For example, in an upcoming meeting agenda, you can include a few minutes for one or two colleagues to explain what they do first when assigned a new project and why.

18. Ask questions in the interest of seeking to understand a person's professional (or personal) experience.

Make an intentional effort to appreciate others' professional and personal experiences. Your genuine curiosity conveys respect and interest in their journeys. For example, in work conversations, ask George to share what his experience was like as a first-time project lead on the team with the employees from the west coast office. In non-work conversations, when your colleague, Nanci, mentions the upcoming Jewish holiday Rosh Hashanah, ask her to tell you about what it signifies.

19. Ask a colleague a question that taps into their knowledge.

Put your coworker in a position to be helpful by simply providing a response to your question. Many employees feel appreciated and valued when they can offer an answer to your question or a solution to your problem off the top of their head.

For example, when my employer, Learn.com, was acquired, I became the resident expert on my new team about the Learn.com system and training programs. I was happy when coworkers asked me questions about the systems or programs because I was able to contribute helpful knowledge.

20. Ask a colleague or leader for their advice.

Many people are flattered and appreciate it when someone thinks highly enough of them to ask them for advice. If you're dealing with a situation, work-related or not, ask yourself, "Who here is the go-to person for X?" Even if you don't know them well, approach them and ask if they'd be willing to speak with you for five to ten minutes at a convenient time to advise you about X. Have your two or three questions ready, honor their time, and be sure to thank them.

Establish Respectful Team Norms or Practices

Be purposeful about and committed to how you work together.

21. Have a team discussion about work style preferences.

Discuss what you can do as a team to honor each other's preferences as you work to balance schedules, meetings, and project deadlines. Understanding how and when your colleagues do their best work respects others' work styles. Awareness of everyone's optimal work styles and rhythms for their workday can guide how and when teamwork and individual work gets done.

For example, at an upcoming team meeting, discuss the time of day when you do your best "deep focus work" or "deep dive thinking." If you discover many of you do your best deep work in the morning, you can schedule project meetings in the afternoon. Similarly, if your team is split in its preferences, you can vary your meeting schedule to accommodate everyone.

22. Discuss and regularly revisit your team's communication practices.

When it comes to communicating with colleagues, when should you text, DM, email, Slack, or call? These guidelines play an integral role in honoring team members' time and attention. Even if your team has previously answered these questions, revisit and reevaluate your answers regularly.

In her Forbes article, "How to Strengthen Remote Teams Through Team Practices," Melissa Daimler, author of *Reculturing: Design Your Company Culture to Connect with Strategy and Purpose for Lasting Success*, recommends discussing the topics below to help teams be more productive.[30] The article focuses on remote teams, but the questions are equally relevant for in-person and hybrid teams.

- What are our expectations around response times?
- What kind of issue or question warrants a call versus a Slack message?

- What are the guidelines for team members' work/life boundaries?[31]

23. Establish a routine practice of discussing workloads and asking for help.

Normalize talking about workloads and the notion of saying, "I need help." Overwhelm is a major contributing factor to burnout at work. Honor your team's well-being by being proactive in alleviating the burden of asking for help.

Reframe asking for help by adding discussion time to meetings where every person completes the phrase, "One task (or project) I could use help with is…" In this way, the expectation is set for everyone to identify an area in which their colleagues can offer support.

24. Give others the leeway to complete assigned or delegated tasks their own way.

When assigning tasks to team members, they may feel micromanaged or not trusted if they're told to complete a task a specific way. It can be belittling to be told exactly how to do something they already know how to do, and they may feel their skills are not valued. Having the agency to perform their responsibilities in the way they see fit demonstrates respect for their skills and knowledge.

Give them the guidelines and expectations for the task and then provide them with the autonomy to do it their way, not yours.

25. Delegate the ability to make decisions without having to run them by you first.

Give your colleagues or project team members the power to make decisions within their realm as a way of demonstrating your trust in their decision-making abilities. It can be demoralizing to run every single decision by your boss or project leader. Of course, some decisions do require your approval.

Provide clear guidelines regarding the decisions that are within their scope and when they need your input. Trust their judgment and ability to make sound choices.

Download all 25 ideas to show
you respect your colleagues:
www.BelongingEnergy.com

Outcomes When We *Respect*

When employees know that their skills and contributions are valued by their organization and recognized by colleagues and leaders, they engage their talent to make even more significant contributions. As Gregg Ward, author of *The Respectful Leader*, points out, employees who feel respected are more likely to:

- work hard, remain loyal, and go the extra mile for their team and/or the company
- be more respectful to their colleagues, leaders, and customers
- have high levels of trust on their teams

> **"I have faith in her. She can do this."**
>
> "When I was tapped for a management position at another research center, other supervisors asked my boss, 'Why are you sending Mira there? She's clueless, she's too young, she's not qualified.'
>
> "My boss, in front of me, would always say, 'I have faith in her. She can do this.'
>
> "And I did. At the research center, I worked hard to earn their trust. As I did, people slowly started to work more effectively together, rebuilding their trust in each other and in the organization. They saw a glimmer of hope. My boss respected me and my capabilities. I, in turn, worked to show my new staff that I respected them and modeled how to respect each other. Their trust in each other influenced their mutual respect."
>
> —Mira

Mira's story illustrates the lasting and significant impact *respect* can have on individuals and organizations. As a result of her professional accomplishments, Mira has had many women ask her, "How did you do it?" She has mentored many other women who are in the beginning stages of their careers. To share what she learned with as many people as possible, she authored the book, *Millennials' Guide to Workplace Politics: What No One Ever Told You About Power and Influence.*

Reflection

When we reflect on what we are learning and apply it to our own lives, our learning deepens, and we are more likely to act on what we learn. These reflection questions invite you to think about your own experiences with respect at work.

1. What's one thing someone at work did to you or for you recently that made you feel your time, talents, and/or contributions were respected and valued?

2. Think back to a situation or experience in your work life when you felt ignored, unseen, or unvalued. Describe the situation. What made this experience memorable for you?

3. What thoughts did you have and how did you feel when it happened?

4. What lessons did you learn from this experience? How have they impacted who you are today?

5. Consider the people you work with: who might be feeling disrespected or not respected right now? Choose one of the ideas from the *respect* category to recognize their talents and contributions. Which spark will you use?

WHAT'S ONE THING YOU LEARNED RECENTLY?

Who is someone you've learned something from recently? What did you learn from them and why does it stand out for you?

Will you "pass it forward" to someone who deserves *respect* by letting them know?

From *Respect* to *Protect*

In the opening story at the beginning of the chapter, Michael described how much it meant to him that his colleagues noticed and appreciated his work. Recognition in the form of a hand-traced high five made him feel respected by his colleagues.

To feel a sense of Belonging at work, employees need to know that their peers and leaders respect their talents and contributions. Employees who feel respected are more productive and engaged. As Michael's story demonstrates, showing your colleagues that you *respect* them is not complicated. Simple ideas like a hand-traced high five say "I respect you" loud and clear.

Now that the values of *connect* and *respect* have been discussed, in the next section, we will explore how *protect* contributes to Belonging at work.

PART SIX

PROTECT

Employees need to feel safe to be and express themselves freely without fear of judgment or exclusion.

Connected

to the people we work
with, our leaders, and
the organization

Respected

by the people we work
with and our leaders

Protected

by the promise that we
are safe to be and to
express ourself freely

WHY PROTECTION MATTERS

Johnna's Story

"Respectful pushback was supported."

"At its worst, my office was a cutthroat place plagued with mistrust. From coworkers all the way up through the leadership, no one trusted anyone. But when the new manager and Board came in, they really respected the staff. They wanted to hear other voices, and they wanted people to tell them what they were thinking. It became an environment where we were encouraged to speak freely and openly. It took a while for the organization to become comfortable with respectful pushback and for it to be supported. Eventually, questions were no longer seen as challenging people, but seeking to understand. Questions were no longer a sign of distrust; they were a sign of curiosity, and that created a much safer space.

"We'd moved back into a space where it was clear that everybody was working for good and for things that would make an impact that improved the quality of life. I felt so much more fulfilled in what I was doing!"

—Johnna

Introduction

Johnna's experience illustrates the power of a healthy, trusting workplace community where colleagues can ask questions and speak their mind without fear of negative consequences. The new leadership at Johnna's company not only respected employees, but they also cultivated a community where speaking up was encouraged. Employees no longer feared that their comments would be misconstrued as criticism. When employees feel protected, they are more productive, engaged, and, as Johnna says, "fulfilled." Their work has more meaning and can have a greater impact on the organization at large.

What *Protect* Means

Humans are imperfect beings. Work communities are rich with talents, and they are also filled with individuals who are afraid their flaws may have negative consequences. To feel a sense of Belonging at work, employees need to trust that their colleagues and leaders will not exploit their weaknesses or vulnerabilities. Your colleagues need to know that you will honor their humanity, and that it's okay to be imperfect, to make mistakes, and to fail occasionally. They want to know that they are safe to use their voice to contribute, to question why and how decisions are made, to ask questions, and to speak candidly.

The third factor that contributes to our sense of belonging at work is feeling the people you work with will *protect* you, which entails being part of a workplace community where trust is strong, communication is honest and transparent, and fair decisions are made. In short, employees are protected by an environment of psychological safety.

Protect is closely related to psychological safety. Amy Edmondson has been instrumental in bringing the idea and importance of psychological safety at work to the forefront of discussions about organizational effectiveness. She defines psychological safety as *"a belief that one will not be punished or humiliated for speaking up with ideas, questions, concerns or mistakes, and that the team is safe for interpersonal risk-taking."*[32] *Protect* results when a workplace community honors the humanness of its members and colleagues trust and respect each other.

In her book *The Fearless Organization*, Edmondson describes how teams that work in environments that are emotionally and psychologically safe yield higher levels of performance because employees are allowed to be themselves without holding back and without fear of retribution.[33] In a well-known research study referred to as "Project Aristotle," Google examined what makes for effective teams. The People Analytics team at Google found that psychological safety was by far the most important dynamic contributing to team effectiveness.[34]

IS IT SAFE TO FAIL IN YOUR WORKPLACE COMMUNITY?

"The biggest factor in promoting innovation is creating this sense of safety, where people feel like they can fail. They try new things because they are not afraid. I can absolutely testify to the fact that if you create that safety, you promote more new ideas and more innovation than environments where people are operating in fear."

—Luis Morales, Executive Director,
Duke University's Master of Engineering Management Program

How do you promote psychological safety with your coworkers and in your organization?

Protect Our Well-Being and Our Time

The primary contributors to employees feeling protected and safe at work are not lofty or unattainable. On the contrary, and not surprisingly, the behaviors that contribute to *protect* center around fairness, mutual trust, and respectful and open communication. As I examined the responses in the *Belonging at Work Survey*© for the behaviors that contribute to a sense of protection, I was surprised to find two additional patterns related to well-being and time emerged:

First, employees feel *protected* when their well-being is not solely their own priority, it's also their team's, leaders', and organization's priority. The focus on well-being isn't new, but the pandemic and surge in remote work environments have heightened its importance as the lines between work and non-work life continue to blur. Employees want their well-being protected. Employees want their workplace communities to support essential time needed to recharge and renew mental energy.

Second, employees want their time *protected*: Adam Grant and his colleagues found that employees spend as much as 80% of their time at work in collaborative activities like meetings, phone calls, and managing emails.[35] That leaves precious little time to produce actual work, let alone the focused think-time needed to produce quality work. This happens when we are not intentional about scheduling meetings or who we invite to them. Employees need time during the workday or week to focus. Honoring a colleague's time contributes to them feeling protected because we are being intentional about making demands on it.

Prioritizing employees' well-being and time are paramount to preventing burnout. In their recent study of burnout, one of the largest studies to date, Gallup found:

The Five Biggest Sources of Burnout:

- Unfair treatment at work
- An unmanageable workload
- Unclear communication from managers
- Lack of support from managers
- Unreasonable time pressure[36]

All of these sources contribute to feeling unprotected at work and fuel employee burnout.

Defining *Protect*

These themes were reiterated in the results of the *Belonging at Work Survey*© and interviews.

As individuals, what we need to feel protected is unique to each one of us. As humans and employees, people feel protected and psychologically safe in their workplace community when they can:

- express themselves freely and completely.
- receive equitable and manageable workloads.
- voice honest opinions and perspectives without fear of retaliation or being shot down, even those that are unpopular or come from different points of view.

Examples from Interviews and Belonging at Work Survey© Responses	
When employees have...	**They respond or feel...**
Trusting, supportive relationships	"I feel protected at work when I feel like my coworkers have my back, and I can ask for help when I need it."
Honest and transparent communication	"I feel safe when my leader is willing to be transparent and let me know he doesn't have an answer. I trust him more because he's honest with me."
Ideas and opinions that are considered by and for everyone	"I feel vulnerable or unprotected at work when my concerns and ideas are brushed aside as unimportant."

When *Protection* Is Missing

When employees don't feel safe to raise concerns, questions, or to speak up about a mistake, the negative consequences can be far-reaching for individuals, teams, and organizations. From the organization perspective, risks include:

- increased turnover
- decreased productivity
- stifled innovation
- lower profitability

Feeling vulnerable or unprotected at work can have a significant impact on the individual as well. Consider Melony's story below.

"I was moved to the call center. On paper, this looks like such a great progression, but it was really a setup."

"I left the distribution center and was moved to the call center. On paper, this looks like such a great progression, but it was really a setup. The culture on this side of the business was worse. Much worse.

"When I came on board, it was known that the call center needed a strong training program. Claudine, who was running the call center program, had been with the company for several years. She'd started at the company as a call center representative when she was in high school and was promoted to run the training program because she was a good rep. I was taking over the program to strengthen it using my education and training experience. But the operations manager didn't tell Claudine ahead of time that I was taking over, so she felt like the program was ripped away from her. By me. She was pissed. She was a mean girl, and she turned the call center into a mean environment. During my last few months, I remember crying in my car, not wanting to go inside. It was awful."

—Melony

A Different Research Approach

To identify the behaviors that make employees feel safe and protected at work, I looked at *protect* from a different angle. **Instead of asking "what makes you feel protected at work," I asked "what makes you feel vulnerable or unprotected at work?"** I wanted to shed light on situations and behaviors employees and leaders may not be aware of that make others feel unprotected. This *Belonging at Work Survey©* prompt reads, "I feel unprotected or vulnerable at work when…" This prompt consistently leads to powerful, sensitive, candid discussions in organizations.

I love the transformative work I do with organizations, especially when we explore what contributes to employees feeling emotionally safe at work. Partnering alongside employees at all levels to identify the behaviors that build and inhibit Belonging always produces fascinating insights. When participants see quotes from their own colleagues, leaders, and/or direct reports, the energy shift is palpable. It is transformative and eye-opening when participants see what makes their own colleagues feel unprotected and vulnerable.

One of the most powerful experiences I've had in my consulting work was with a technology company. A group of twenty-five employees from across the organization participated in the program, completing the *Belonging at Work Survey©* in preparation for the first meeting. During the program, when we discussed their survey responses, it felt like the air was sucked out of the room when this response was displayed on the PowerPoint slide: *"I feel unprotected at work when others are hostile towards me in a meeting, and no one says anything about it."* The room was silent. There it was: a big bullying elephant in the room.

This single response sparked a much-needed, candid discussion about balancing respect for individual expression (a company value) and acceptable behavior towards others. The leaders in the room saw the impact the person was having on employees. Coworkers also saw the impact their choice to remain silent was having on their colleagues. No one could ignore the impact of unchecked inappropriate behavior. As a result of the discussion, everyone present committed to speaking up when someone becomes hostile or bullying in a meeting.

> "The further up I went in the organization, the less protected I felt."
>
> —Johnna

While everyone has unique experiences with what contributes to them feeling vulnerable in their workplace communities, there are common themes. Below are ten common themes that emerged from the *Belonging at Work Survey*© responses. How many of these sound familiar to you?

Ten Common Situations Where Employees Feel *Unprotected* at Work

"I feel vulnerable or unprotected at work when…"

1. …I struggle to complete my work.
2. …my input, opinions, or ideas are dismissed.
3. …I hear them talking about other employees behind their backs.
4. …they don't stand up for me.
5. …we are expected to take on the work of colleagues who were laid off without additional support or extended deadlines.
6. …I am not given a voice in decisions made about my work, priorities, or workload.
7. …someone on my team is criticized in public during a meeting.
8. …company needs are prioritized over our human needs.
9. …my leaders don't follow through on what they say.
10. …I make a mistake.

Which of these sound familiar to you?

Belonging at Work Survey© Results

It's not just colleagues who contribute to employees feeling vulnerable. Leaders can also make employees feel unprotected.

"She used to mark up my reports with a red pen."

"I grew up in Puerto Rico. I learned to read English, but conversational English was not something I learned in school. In my first job, I was still struggling with my spoken and written English. Conversations with my supervisor, Patty, were really painful for me because she would shove my language mistakes in my face. She used to mark up my reports with a red pen. The recurring theme she kept going back to was that I 'wasn't [company name] material, that I didn't belong there, that this job was for people who are up here, and I was way down here.'

"This situation was eating me up inside. I thought to myself, 'What did I do wrong?' I was a student leader, and an honors student in college with a lot of friends. Now, all of a sudden, I am inept, and I don't belong. I wondered, 'Is it me? There must be something I'm doing.'

"After about three months of daily humiliation, I was in a one-on-one meeting with her. She was on one of her diatribes and I got angry. I told her, 'I know what you want. You want me to quit. I promise you, no matter how painful you make it for me, I will never quit. Ever. So you keep at it.' And then I became quiet. She started smirking, smiling. She said, 'That's what I was looking for! What took you so long to push back?' She didn't change after that, but I felt I was in more control of my reality."

—Luis

Examples of *Protect*

When I consult with learning and development professionals to identify behaviors that foster workplace communities where employees feel protected, their responses are eye-opening. They provide key insights into the influence that support (or lack thereof) has on employees. For example, one talent development professional responded, "I feel unprotected at work when my coworkers and leader ignore my plea for help on a high-profile project."

Feeling protected at work is essential and a powerful factor in creating a sense of Belonging. Small, simple actions can contribute the most to feeling protected.

While everyone has unique experiences with Belonging, there are common characteristics individuals mention as examples of workplace communities where they feel protected. The examples below represent several of the themes that emerged from the interviews and *Belonging at Work Survey*© responses, including frequent and honest communication, transparency, and supportive relationships built on trust. How many of these sound familiar to you?

Ten Common Ways to *Protect*

"I feel protected by my colleagues and leaders at work when..."

1. ...I am included in decision-making that affects me, my team, or my project.
2. ...we can speak openly and candidly about things that are going well and things that are not.
3. ...we honor each other's well-being by respecting work/home boundaries.
4. ...we don't criticize each other when we make mistakes.
5. ...we ensure open and consistent communication, so others are not left out or blindsided by changes or new information.
6. ...one or more colleagues offer to help before I even ask for it.
7. ...we jointly decide to adjust project deadlines to release time pressure.
8. ...my leader highlights my contributions to their leaders.
9. ...leaders live up to their commitments by doing what they say they would.
10. ...we objectively discuss things that are not going smoothly on the team.

Which of these sound familiar to you?

Belonging at Work Survey© Results

25 Simple Ideas to *Protect* Your Colleagues

Employees feel protected when they are supported by trusting relationships with frequent and honest communication. Over 1,500 *Belonging at Work Survey*© responses indicate that employees feel protected when their workloads are distributed fairly and their well-being is prioritized.

What can employees do to show their coworkers and team members the sense of safety they deserve and crave? Below are twenty-five simple ideas to protect your colleagues and create a workplace community that honors everyone's humanness. My hope is that you will see how simple these ideas are and that they inspire ideas for you. While they may not all work for your organization, I am confident many of them will. Discuss and adapt them to use with peers, team members, and colleagues in other departments or groups. They can be used in person and virtually. Get creative: experiment with modifying them to add your own spark!

Create a Safe Space

Foster an environment where your colleagues feel comfortable being who they are.

1. Honor all emotions.

On any given day, humans experience a wide range of emotions, but many work environments are not supportive of employees being anything other than "fine." Honoring each other's state of mind conveys it is safe to express all of who you are. Set an example of accepting your colleagues wherever they are emotionally and making it okay to have a bad day or to not be "fine" right now. Honor and embrace your colleagues' and your own well-being by acknowledging and accepting the less happy emotions or mental states along with the positive ones.

2. Model that it's safe to be vulnerable by sharing something personal.

Contribute to the sense of trust and transparency on your team or in your group by being the first to be vulnerable. By modeling a willingness to risk being seen as imperfect or as someone who makes mistakes, you foster an environment where your colleagues can feel safe to be human, too. What you choose to share doesn't have to be huge. It can be a question you didn't have an answer to in a client meeting or a decision you struggled to make.

3. Release the burden of failures.

Making a mistake can produce intense shame and fear of harsh judgment from leaders and colleagues. Relieve the anxiety associated with errors by fostering a supportive environment where they can be shared without blame or judgment. This kind of compassionate culture conveys that it is safe to make mistakes on your team.

Host an occasional "Facepalm Friday" (or any other day) where colleagues share their latest professional or personal error or snafu. The opportunity to unburden mistakes in a non-judgmental atmosphere will work wonders for creating a space filled with emotional safety.

4. Host "Question Time"

Many employees are uncomfortable asking questions because they are afraid of being judged or they think they should know the answer. Be proactive in alleviating that fear by creating an open time for colleagues to ask questions about anything. Creating a space for your colleagues to ask questions reassures them that questions are expected and welcome.

For example, include ten minutes for "Question Time" on your team meeting agenda once a month. Depending on your group culture, employees may ask questions in real time or submit questions ahead of the meeting. Similarly, questions may be asked anonymously, or not.

5. Acknowledge and apologize for your mistakes.

It can be challenging to acknowledge it publicly or to concede to others when you make a mistake. However, acknowledging your own mess-up demonstrates a standard of transparency and that it is safe to make a mistake. Hold yourself accountable for contributing to the compassionate environment you want to work in by acknowledging when you've erred. Offer a sincere apology by recognizing what happened, explaining what you learned from the situation, and sharing your solution or plan to remedy the situation.

Champion Others

Be a compassionate advocate, cheerleader, and guardian for your colleagues.

6. Grant grace and forgiveness to others.

Offering and receiving forgiveness and grace are essential elements that protect a workplace community. Sometimes others' words or actions can rub us the wrong way, or a colleague's failure to foresee a challenging issue can frustrate us because of the additional work it creates. When your colleagues acknowledge and apologize for their mistakes, extend the same grace and forgiveness you hope they will offer you when the mistake is yours. Your reaction demonstrates compassion is a value in your community.

7. Recognize the people who contribute to a project to ensure they get credit for their contributions.

When you are discussing a project's success in meetings with others (especially leaders) or one-on-one conversations, be sure to name the individuals who contributed to the project. Acknowledging others and shining a positive light on their talents increases their visibility within the organization and demonstrates you care enough about them to make sure they receive well-deserved recognition.

In discussions about projects, mention by name a few of the people who have made a significant impact. If someone else is discussing a project and a person is left out of the recognition list, add the person's name so their contributions are recognized as well.

8. Advocate for and recognize your colleagues.

Like recognizing others' contributions to a specific project, acknowledging the positive impact your colleagues are having in other areas of the organization also showcases their contributions and increases their visibility.

In meetings with your leaders and others, share the positive feedback you hear from a client about your coworker. Advocate for your colleagues by speaking up for them when they are neck-deep in work. For example, if you know Mark is on a tight deadline, speak up for him when Keith suggests Mark would be a great person to lead an upcoming onsite client meeting.

9. Encourage a "Yes, and..." approach to brainstorming.

Adopt a supportive approach to collaboration and brainstorming by adopting the "Yes, and..." technique. It's an approach to discussions that ensure colleagues' ideas are supported by affirming and adding on to them. It conveys all ideas are worth exploring and encourages your colleagues to openly contribute to discussions without fear of criticism. This technique shortcuts the human tendency to focus first on the reasons an idea will not work by removing the word "but" and opening the door for more new ideas.

Point out a viable piece of coworker's recommendation or idea. As Rachel Peck describes in her article, "5 Ways the 'Yes, And' Improv Technique Can Help You at Work—While Protecting Your Boundaries," the "yes, and" technique guides us to listen deeply to others, affirm their reality, and build upon their perspective.[37]

10. Speak directly to the person with whom you have an issue.

If you have a concern or a gripe about a colleague's behavior or a decision they made, commit to yourself to speak to the person directly without talking behind their back. Being proactive and straightforward with others builds trust, communicates you value the relationships you have at work, and shows your commitment to maintaining healthy bonds.

Seek guidance and counsel from a trusted advisor first if you need to, but do not feed the gossip monster by talking *about* them rather than *to* the person directly.

Create Transparent Communication Practices

Model a commitment to communicate with transparency.

11. Communicate often and effectively, providing information that is safe to share.

With so much change and uncertainty in today's workplaces, employees are concerned about being out of the loop. Sometimes, in a well-intentioned effort to provide answers and reduce their coworkers' uncertainty, project leaders or employees with information wait until they have concrete answers before updating their team. In the meantime, though, the team frets in silence and anxious uncertainty. Their effort to reduce uncertainty by waiting until they have some concrete details to share instead induces anxiety.

Many of us are reluctant to say, "I don't know," but transparency builds more trust than silence. If you are able to share information with your team, tell them what is appropriate for you to share with them. Let them ask candid questions. Answer the ones you can and give them your best insight based on what you know.

12. Facilitate a discussion about your team's communication practices.

Discuss communication preferences to create clear, shared understanding about expected response times and communication channels. Team members have different expectations when it comes to communication. Coming to an agreement about what practices are acceptable creates trust and transparency within your team.

For example, some people keep instant messaging apps open throughout the day. They don't mind being interrupted by notifications for new messages and may respond to messages immediately. Other coworkers don't use instant messaging at all or only open it as needed. Having clear expectations for and understanding about how you communicate creates healthy team practices.

13. Host team discussions about what is going well and what can go better.

Schedule regular times to have open, candid discussions about what your group, team, or department is doing well and where there is room for improvement. This discussion on a quarterly or per project basis provides an opportunity to celebrate your successes, evaluate schedules, and adjust deadlines and expectations, which strengthens mutual trust within your team. Set the expectation of transparency and candor in these discussions by guiding everyone to bring up at least one team brag, one team snag, and one recommendation.

14. Foster visibility for your remote colleagues.

Many employees in remote or hybrid work environments are concerned that they are missing out on discussions and career opportunities because they are not physically in the office. One way to ease their concern and demonstrate you have their back is to create opportunities for your remote colleagues to be seen and heard by those in the office.

For example, one of my clients arranged for their team to rotate the responsibility for facilitating the monthly meetings with senior leadership so remote team members were visible to senior leaders and remained on their radar.

15. Loop someone into a relevant communication thread.

The simple act of bringing a colleague into the fold shows you are looking out for them and ensuring they are included in relevant communications.

For example, if you and Ted are working on the new client experience project and you realize he was not included on the last email exchange discussing changes in the delivery schedule, forward the email to him or include him when you respond.

Confront Inappropriate Behavior

Create a safe environment by showing your colleagues that unacceptable behavior will not be tolerated.

16. Address behavior that violates agreed upon team norms.

Defining team norms regarding work schedules, communication practices, and how the team does its work can prevent a lot of misunderstandings and potential conflicts. Team norms serve as guidelines demonstrating how the members of a group have agreed to work together. When someone does not live up to the agreements they've made, it is essential to address their behavior and call them back into alignment with team norms.

One way to bring up the topic is in a private discussion. In a one-on-one conversation, describe their behavior, then ask them to help you understand what happened and for their perspective of the situation.

17. Do not allow rude or disrespectful behavior to go unchecked.

Employees and leaders have a shared responsibility to provide a safe environment at work. Even if behavior is not "technically" over the line, there still comes a time when a behavior is impolite and inconsiderate. Protect the psychological safety of your work community by calling out any rude behavior you witness.

You don't have to confront the person publicly. Instead, speak to them privately about what was said or done that was disrespectful and its potential impact. Ask them to help you understand the situation from their perspective.

18. Stand up when you hear people making disrespectful comments about a colleague or having inappropriate conversations.

Regardless of your role in the organization, when you allow disrespectful comments about a colleague to go unchecked, you support an unsafe workplace environment. When you diplomatically address those who are making disparaging remarks, you build trust and respect. You don't have to be aggressive or confrontational. You can say something like, "I find this discussion inappropriate and disrespectful. I am not going to be a part of it."

What is deemed an "inappropriate conversation" varies from one organization or setting to another. Of course, some situations may require a more formal response, such as reporting them to your manager or HR.

19. Stand up for the person who is interrupted while speaking.

It is disrespectful to interrupt a person when they are speaking. When you address an interrupter, you convey that the person who has the floor is respected and that you will protect the floor for them.

This idea is also a way to demonstrate respect and is described in more detail in the *Respect* section (see Respect Idea #13). It is included here as well because it was a common response on the *Belonging at*

Work survey prompt that asks about behaviors that make employees feel vulnerable or unprotected at work.

Here are a few examples of what you might say in this situation:

- "Excuse me, Dan, let's let Michael finish what he was saying."
- "Hold on tight, Dan. Michael, finish your thought."
- "Dan, hang on to your thought while Michael finishes his."

20. Refuse to participate in office gossip.

Office gossip does not serve any healthy purpose. It erodes trust. When coworkers hear you feed the rumor mill, talking about what you heard someone say in the elevator, you share information that is not yours to share, and it may not be true. They may wonder whether they can trust you to keep a conversation confidential or whether you will gossip about them as well.

Do not gossip. Honor the trust your colleagues place in you when they tell you something in confidence. Do not share any information that is not yours to share.

Here are some examples of what to do or say when you hear gossip:

- Walk away.
- "That's not my business."
- "I am not comfortable talking about that."

Commit to Protecting Well-Being

Foster an environment that prioritizes health and well-being.

21. Encourage others to take energy breaks.

We all benefit from a brief change of scenery, like leaving our desks, standing up, and taking a brief walk to recharge mentally and physically.

Bodies, brains, and butts need to be shaken out and refreshed to do our best work.

Support your colleagues' mental and physical well-being by encouraging them to get a change of scenery, to not eat at their desks, and to take movement breaks throughout the day. Change your scenery together with a quick walk!

22. Monitor the number of "yeses" given to keep track of their commitments.

Prioritize and guard your project team members' time commitments to ensure they have energy to focus on the projects aligned with the team's and organization's goals and values. For example, Simone, a team leader, leads a high-performing team of individuals who enjoy being called upon to help at work. She sees herself as a guardian of her team's energy levels and uses the strategy described below to manage their energy to prevent burnout.

If she sees John make a commitment that raises her eyebrows, she'll ask him, with genuine curiosity, "John, is this project something you need to be working on? And does it really need to be done by Tuesday?" She respects his response and stands by him if he changes his commitment. As a result of her monitoring, Simone's team members have improved their ability to say "no" more often and say "yes" to commitments that honor their energy.

It is important to note that Simone's practice comes from a place of protecting the team's energy and mental focus. It is not micromanaging or criticizing a team member's commitments. It's clear from conversations with her team that they trust her perspective and do not feel micromanaged.

23. Balance your team's and your own schedules with time to recharge.

Research shows that sustaining attention and mental focus consumes cognitive resources that require rest to replenish them. It is mentally exhausting to transition directly from one project or meeting to the next without taking time to recharge the brain, body, and mind. Be intentional about scheduling time buffers for yourself and your colleagues. Provide an opportunity to recharge their brains and catch up on tasks before shifting focus to the next project.

Here are a few examples of buffer time for yourself and your coworkers:

- Schedule a buffer of one to three days between the completion of one project and the start of another one.
- Limit meeting times to fifteen, twenty-five, or forty-five minutes so attendees have time for a break before their next meeting.
- Schedule a recharging event to celebrate a major project or team milestone.

24. Ensure your team members and colleagues take their paid time off so they can recharge.

Team members need time off to recharge. More than ever today, employees are pushed to work harder and longer. Taking time off may feel impossible, but the more impossible it seems, the more it is needed! Time away from work is essential to achieve and maintain well-being. Making sure your coworkers (and you) take time off demonstrates that you honor their (and your) well-being.

For example, to safeguard their team members' well-being, several of my clients have found the need to shift from "*encouraging*" team members to take time off to "*expecting*" they take it.

25. Honor your colleagues' work/home boundaries.

By supporting your colleagues' boundaries, you are encouraging their efforts to practice self-care and demonstrating trust. Hybrid and remote environments mean employees' guardrails between work and non-work are blurrier than ever. Receiving emails after the workday ends or before it starts contributes to overwhelm and burnout.

One way to honor work/home boundaries is to commit to sending emails during the recipient's work hours. Microsoft Outlook and Google's Gmail have features that allow you to compose an email but delay its delivery, so you can write the email at your convenience and schedule it to automatically be delivered during the recipient's work hours.

Download all 25 ideas to
protect your colleagues:
www.BelongingEnergy.com

Outcomes When We *Protect*

Employees are more creative and innovative when they feel safe to be human. As Luis Morales from Duke University mentioned, an environment where it is okay to fail produces more new and creative ideas than a workplace community where employees operate in fear.

It's not just the organization that benefits from an environment where employees feel *protected*. In a safe community, individuals can grow in life-changing ways.

One of my most rewarding experiences so far teaching at Duke happened during my first semester as an adjunct professor. In one class, we discussed whether introverts can be leaders (the answer is "Yes!") and the differences between introversion and shyness. After class, a student of mine, Vijay, approached me. He said, "Professor, can you help me? I am uncomfortable making small talk with people. I just don't like it. But my work study job at the gym requires me to talk to people. I don't know what to say."

I suggested he come up with three questions that he can ask that will tell him something he would find interesting about them, and they would be happy to elaborate on, which means they would carry the conversation and he would not have to talk as much. For example,

Vijay is passionate about fitness, so I suggested he might ask them what one of their fitness goals is or whether they were targeting a muscle group during their workout that day. By the way, when he asks them about their fitness goals, he shows interest in them, which is *connection*! (Belonging is not just for employees. It's also a way to provide superior customer service!)

After the last class that semester, Vijay approached me, grinning from ear to ear. This shy, low-key young man was overflowing with excitement and pride. He said, "Thank you, Professor. Your advice has changed my life. You helped me see that I had an inner belief that said, 'you are not good at talking to people.' I realized it was wrong! I do like talking to people and I'm good at it now! Now, if you go to the gym, and ask, 'where's Vijay?' everyone will be able to direct you to me because everyone knows me. I want you to know that I was voted 'Employee of the Month.' Thank you."

I worked hard to make my classroom a place where students felt safe, even the introverted and shy ones who were reluctant or down-right scared to speak in front of others. Vijay confirmed to me that my efforts that semester to create a classroom where students felt *protected* paid off.

Reflection

When we reflect on what we are learning and apply it to our own lives, our learning deepens, and we are more likely to act on what we learn. These reflection questions are an invitation to think about your own experiences with feeling safe or vulnerable at work.

1. What's one thing someone at work did to you or for you recently that made you feel safe and protected?

2. Think back to a situation or experience in your work life when you felt particularly vulnerable, exposed, and/or unprotected. Describe the situation. What happened that made this experience memorable for you?

3. What thoughts did you have and what did you feel when it happened?

4. What lessons did you learn from this experience? How have they impacted who you are today?

5. Consider the people you work with: who might be feeling unprotected right now? Choose one of the *protect* ideas to reassure them. Which spark will you use?

Where Do We Go from Here?

The opening story shared how Johnna's work community changed dramatically for the better under new leadership. She mentioned the marked improvement in their ability to communicate openly and freely and how the shift in how they saw (and received) respectful pushback and questions transformed their work environment. It changed from a place of deep mistrust where everyone focused on protecting their own power and ideas to one that flourished, as it was able to shift focus to making a positive impact on the quality of life in their larger community.

Workplace communities foster Belonging by encouraging transparency and trust so employees can ask questions without fear about how they will be perceived. As Johnna's experience highlighted, these work cultures unify employees and steer them toward a united goal. Simple actions, such as ensuring all relevant parties are invited to meetings, contribute to a sense of safety and protection at work.

We've explored the strong community that results when employees feel *connected*, *respected*, and *protected* at work. In the next section, we bring it all together and discuss what comes next.

PART SEVEN

SUMMARY

FINAL THOUGHTS

Ken's Lightbulb Moment: It's That Simple

"It's that simple, isn't it?" Ken asked me, holding a "You Belong Here" sticker in front of him with the expression of someone who'd made an astonishing discovery. His question touched my soul because it showed me he got it. Ken realized that something as small and simple as a sticker can build belonging in his workplace community.

He was holding a Pride version of the "You Belong Here" sticker. He'd just picked it up at the conclusion of "the Energy of Belonging" training program I facilitated at his organization. The stickers are one of my gifts to program participants to keep Belonging on their mind: I give every participant a "You Belong Here" sticker and explain that, as an ally, I extend an intentional, visual message of Belonging specifically for the LGBTQ+ community with a Pride version of the sticker. Anyone who wants one is invited to see me after the program to get one. Ken, an ally, approached me as he picked up his Pride sticker.

As a career scientist, Ken's natural approach to challenges was scientific: ask questions, make thorough observations, formulate hypotheses, and experiment with various solutions, with the goal of drawing conclusions from the evidence. The Pride version of the sticker sparked Ken's realization that he'd been overcomplicating his own approach to fostering Belonging at work. He realized small, simple actions like putting a sticker on his laptop cover can have a significant impact on his colleagues feeling welcomed.

And so it goes.

We may not be scientists, but like Ken, many of us also overcomplicate our approach to fostering Belonging in our workplace communities. It is my hope that *The Energy of Belonging* inspires you to simplify yours. Embrace and use the power you have to spark Belonging in your own environment. Equipped with the seventy-five ideas described in these pages and the additional ones inspired by your reflections, you can spark Belonging and reshape the community in which you work.

The Book's Purpose – Revisited

The Energy of Belonging is a belonging resource specifically for employees. It shares ideas from others like your work BFFs and colleagues about what you can do to *connect* with them, demonstrate *respect* for them, and *protect* their well-being. This book empowers you by giving you ways to meet the innate need your colleagues (and all humans) have to feel like they belong. You can now spark a genuine sense of belonging in your colleagues who feel disconnected, dis- or not respected, and unsafe to be themselves.

The Energy of Belonging

"The Energy of Belonging" is the vibe generated by the degree of Belonging within a community. When that vibe is strong, the resulting vitality fuels the group's productivity, creativity, and performance, yielding positive and profitable outcomes. However, when the degree of Belonging within a team is low, the opposite outcomes are produced: reduced productivity, inhibited problem-solving, and lower overall performance. All employees deserve to experience the invigorating, positive energy of belonging. You now have the power to fuel your colleagues' sense of belonging with these simple ideas to *connect* with, *respect*, and *protect* them.

How to *Connect* with Your Colleagues

Belonging at work is fueled by employees feeling connected to their peers, leaders, and their organization. Employees feel like they're a part of their workplace community when they know the people they work with and are known by them. We each have our own definition of connection, but what the definitions have in common is the bond between colleagues that results from knowing each other as human beings, not just as coworkers. Workplace communities where employees feel connected enjoy not only increased engagement and morale but higher quality work output and higher productivity. When connection is missing, the opposite is true: the environment suffers from higher turnover, lower work quality, and more missed workdays.

Responses to the *Belonging at Work Survey*© illuminated that connection does not require substantial, expensive, time-consuming gestures. Instead, it calls for simple, thoughtful interactions, like saying "hello" as a colleague enters the room, sharing laughter, and celebrating milestones together.

The twenty-five ideas to *connect* with your colleagues centered around these five themes:

- Invite individual conversations to get to know others.
- Invigorate others by showing them you are thinking about them.
- Integrate connection activities into team meetings to deepen relationships.
- Initiate events beyond your team to create shared experiences with others outside your immediate team.
- Incorporate play and self-care by creating time for laughter, fun, and well-being.

How to *Respect* Your Colleagues

The second key theme influencing the sense of belonging at work is employees knowing their talents, contributions, and time matter to peers and leaders. Employees feel respected when they know they are appreciated and valued, and others recognize the positive impact their contributions make to the organization. Like *connect*, what *respect* looks like varies for everyone, but the common themes are recognition, autonomy to decide how their work gets done, and invitations to provide input on decisions. Work environments where employees are respected enjoy stronger commitment to organizational goals and employee engagement. When respect is missing, the negative consequences can include withholding essential solutions, "quiet quitting," and a diluted sense of community.

Responses to the *Belonging at Work Survey*© reinforced the idea that showing appreciation and respect does not demand huge, expensive gestures. Instead, employees want small, simple acts of recognition, like being asked for their advice, having their contributions acknowledged, and having their career aspirations discussed.

The twenty-five ideas to *respect* your colleagues were organized into these five themes:

- Engage with others by being fully present with them.
- Ensure people are honored by seeing others as they want to be seen.
- Ensure all voices are heard respectfully.
- Enlist input and expertise by inviting others to share theirs.
- Establish respectful team norms or practices.

How to *Protect* Your Colleagues

The third factor that contributes to the sense of belonging in a workplace community is how protected and safe employees feel to express themselves fully without fear of negative consequences. Employees experience psychological safety when the trust within their environment is strong, communication is candid and honest, and decisions are made fairly and with transparency. Workplace communities where employees feel protected have higher levels of innovation, performance, and team effectiveness. When employees do not feel safe to raise concerns or speak up, the workplace environment suffers from increased turnover, decreased productivity and creativity, and lower profitability.

Responses to the *Belonging at Work Survey*© revealed that employees feel vulnerable or unprotected at work when they hear colleagues talking about other employees behind their backs, when leaders don't follow through on their commitments, and when they don't have a voice in decisions about their work. The survey responses also high-lighted that employees feel protected by their colleagues and leaders when their team does not criticize mistakes, when work/home bound-aries are honored, and when team challenges can be discussed candidly.

The twenty-five ideas to *protect* your colleagues focused on these five themes:

- Create safe spaces where others feel comfortable being who they are.
- Champion others by advocating and cheering for colleagues.
- Create and commit to transparent communication practices.
- Confront inappropriate behavior to demonstrate it will not be tolerated.
- Commit to protecting well-being by prioritizing it.

What's Next? Put an Idea into Action

I challenge you to challenge yourself: choose one idea from each sec-tion and commit to acting on them once within the next thirty days. Choose the easiest ones or the most challenging ones—it doesn't mat-ter which, just choose! And act. I have no doubt you will be pleasantly surprised by the positive impact it has on your own outlook and the impact your intention to connect with, respect, and protect your col-leagues has on them.

Creating the workplace community you and your colleagues will love, where all of you will enjoy a strong sense of belonging, is within reach. Your reach. You have the power, and now, the tools, to cre-ate that space with simple actions that yield an incredible outcome: a thriving workplace community that clearly conveys "You Belong Here" to all.

Please Review the Book

Hey, it's Wendy here.

I hope you've enjoyed the book, finding it both useful and fun. I have a favor to ask you.

Would you please consider giving the book a rating wherever you bought it? Online book stores are more likely to promote a book when they feel good about its content, and reader reviews are a great barometer for a book's quality.

So please go to the website of wherever you bought the book, search for my name and the book title, and leave a review. If you're game, perhaps consider adding a picture of you holding the book. That increases the likelihood your review will be accepted!

Many thanks in advance for your support,

—Wendy Gates Corbett

Will You Please Share the Love?

Get this book for a friend, family member, work BFF, or colleague!

If you were energized by this book and found it valuable, please consider buying a copy for someone else who could use a spark. Special bulk discounts are available if you would like your whole team or organization to benefit from reading this. Just contact Wendy at wendy@ signature-presentations.com.

Would You Like Wendy Gates Corbett to Speak to Your Organization or at Your Conference?

Book Wendy Now!

Wendy accepts a limited number of speaking engagements at international, regional, and organizational events providing keynote presentations, VIP programs, pre-conference workshops, and sessions each year.

To learn how you can bring her transformative message and expertise to your organization, reach out to info@signature-presentations.com or visit wendygatescorbett.com.

ENDNOTES

Part One: You Don't Belong Here! You're Different!

1. Gallup, Inc. *State of the Global Workplace 2023 Report*. Washington, D.C.: Gallup, Inc., 2023. https://www.gallup.com/ workplace/349484/state-of-the-global-workplace.aspx. Accessed August 08, 2023.
2. *Ibid.*

Part Two: Belonging Defined, Explained, and Demonstrated

3. BetterUp. *The Value of Belonging at Work: New Frontiers for Inclusion in 2021 and Beyond*. Austin: BetterUp Labs, 2020. https://f.hubspotusercontent40.net/hubfs/9253440/ Asset%20PDFs/Promotions_Assets_Reports/BetterUp_ BelongingReport_121720.pdf. Accessed August 08, 2023.
4. Cross, Rob, Reb Rebele, and Adam Grant. "Collaborative Overload." *Harvard Business Review*. January-February 2016. https://hbr.org/ 2016/01/collaborative-overload. Accessed August 08, 2023.
5. Tabrizi, Behnam. "75% of Cross-Functional Teams Are Dysfunctional." *Harvard Business Review*, June 23, 2015. https:// hbr.org/2015/06/75-of-cross-functional-teams-are-dysfunctional. Accessed August 08, 2023.
6. BetterUp. *The Value of Belonging at Work: New Frontiers for Inclusion in 2021 and Beyond*. Austin: BetterUp Labs, 2020. https://f.hubspotusercontent40.net/hubfs/9253440/ Asset%20PDFs/Promotions_Assets_Reports/BetterUp_ BelongingReport_121720.pdf. Accessed August 08, 2023.

7. LinkedIn Learning. *2022 Workplace Learning Report: The Transformation of L&D*. Sunnyvale: LinkedIn Corporation, 2022. https://learning.linkedin.com/content/dam/me/learning/resources/pdfs/inkedIn-learning-workplace-learning-report-2022.pdf. Accessed August 08, 2023.

8. Coqual. *The Power of Belonging: What It Is and Why It Matters in Today's Workplace*. New York: Coqual, 2020. https://coqual.org/reports/the-power-of-belonging/. Accessed August 08, 2023.

9. *Ibid.*

Part Three: The Energy of Belonging

10. Clifton, Jon. "The Power of Work Friends." *Harvard Business Review*, October 07, 2022. https://hbr.org/2022/10/the-power-of-work-friends. Accessed August 08, 2023.

11. *Ibid.*

12. Patel, Alok and Stephanie Plowman. "The Increasing Importance of a Best Friend at Work." *Gallup Workplace*, August 17, 2022. https://www.gallup.com/workplace/397058/increasing-importance-best-friend-work.aspx. Accessed August 08, 2023.

13. Ramesh, Archana. "Why Belonging is Important at Work: Employee Engagement and Diversity." Glintinc.com, April 23, 2020. https://www.glintinc.com/blog/why-belonging-is-important-at-work-employee-engagement-and-diversity/. Accessed August 08, 2023.

14. O.C. Tanner Institute. *2023 Global Culture Report*. Salt Lake City: O.C. Tanner Institute, 2023. https://res.cloudinary.com/oct-corp/image/private/s--pTdZnnhF--/v1687983491/website/octanner-global-culture-report-2023.pdf [or https://www.octanner.com/global-culture-report-executive-summary/2023]. Accessed August 08, 2023.

15. BetterUp. *The Value of Belonging at Work: New Frontiers for Inclusion in 2021 and Beyond*. Austin: BetterUp Labs, 2020. https://f.hubspotusercontent40.net/hubfs/9253440/Asset%20PDFs/Promotions_Assets_Reports/BetterUp_BelongingReport_121720.pdf. Accessed August 08, 2023.

Part Four: Connect

16. O.C. Tanner Institute. *2022 Global Culture Report*. Salt Lake City: O.C. Tanner Institute, 2022. https://www.octanner.com/global-culture-report-executive-summary/2022. Accessed August 08, 2023.

17. *Ibid.*

18. DeSmet, Aaron, Bonnie Dowling, Marino Mugayar-Baldocchi, and Bill Schaninger. "Gone for Now, or Gone for Good? How to Play the New Talent Game and Win Back Workers." McKinsey Quarterly. March 09, 2022. https://www.mckinsey.com/capabilities/people-and-organizational-performance/our-insights/gone-for-now-or-gone-for-good-how-to-play-the-new-talent-game-and-win-back-workers. Accessed August 08, 2023.

19. "Professionalism and the 5 Principles." Duke Engineering Management. June 29, 2021. https://memp.pratt.duke.edu/5-principles. Accessed August 08, 2023.

20. Taylor Kennedy, Julia and Pooja Jain-Link. "What Does it Take to Build a Culture of Belonging?" *Harvard Business Review*, June 21, 2021. https://hbr.org/2021/06/what-does-it-take-to-build-a-culture-of-belonging. Accessed August 08, 2023.

21. Coqual. *The Power of Belonging: What It Is and Why It Matters in Today's Workplace*. New York: Coqual, 2020. https://coqual.org/reports/the-power-of-belonging/. Accessed August 08, 2023.

22. Smiley Poswolsky, Adam. "How Leaders Can Build Connection in a Disconnected Workplace." *Harvard Business Review*, January 21, 2022. https://hbr.org/2022/01/how-leaders-can-build-connection-in-a-disconnected-workplace. Accessed August 08, 2023.

23. BetterUp. *The Value of Belonging at Work: New Frontiers for Inclusion in 2021 and Beyond*. Austin: BetterUp Labs, 2020. https://f.hubspotusercontent40.net/hubfs/9253440/Asset%20PDFs/Promotions_Assets_Reports/BetterUp_BelongingReport_121720.pdf. Accessed August 08, 2023.

24. *Ibid.*

25. Cigna Healthcare. *Loneliness and the Workplace: 2020 U.S. Report.* Bloomfield: Cigna, 2020. https://www.cigna.com/static/ www-cigna-com/docs/about-us/newsroom/studies-and-reports/ combatting-loneliness/cigna-2020-loneliness-report.pdf. Accessed August 08, 2023.

26. Brown, Brene. "Connection Comes in Many Different Forms. We Can Even Find Meaning in Being Weary Together." LinkedIn, 2021. https://www.linkedin. com/posts/brenebrown_we-start-every-meeting-with- a-two-word-check-in-activity-6742131171414618112-Dacq/. Accessed August 8, 2023.

27. *New Decade, New Direction.* Tamworth: The Institute of Leadership & Management, 2020. www.institutelm.com/resourceLibrary/ new-decade-new-direction.html. Accessed August 08, 2023.

Part Five: Respect

28. Coqual. *The Power of Belonging: What It Is and Why It Matters in Today's Workplace.* New York: Coqual, 2020. https://coqual.org/ reports/the-power-of-belonging/. Accessed: August 08, 2023.

29. LinkedIn Learning. *2022 Workplace Learning Report: The Transformation of L&D.* Sunnyvale: LinkedIn Corporation, 2022. https://learning.linkedin.com/content/dam/me/learning/ resources/pdfs/linkedIn-learning-workplace-learning-report-2022. pdf. Accessed August 08, 2023.

30. Daimler, Melissa. "How to Strengthen Remote Teams Through Team Practices." Forbes.com, March 26, 2021. https://www.forbes.com/sites/melissadaimler/2021/03/26/ how-to-strengthen-remote-teams-through-team- practices/?sh=7de49942d768. Accessed August 08, 2023.

31. *Ibid.*

Part Six: Protect

32. Edmondson, Amy C. "Psychological Safety." https://amycedmondson.com/psychological-safety/. Accessed August 14, 2023.

33. Edmondson, Amy C. "The Fearless Organization: Creating Psychological Safety in the Workplace for Learning, Innovation, and Growth." Hoboken: John Wiley & Sons, Inc., 2019.

34. Charles Duhigg, "What Google Learned from Its Quest to Build the Perfect Team." *The New York Times,* February 25, 2016. https://www.nytimes.com/2016/02/28/magazine/what-google-learned-from-its-quest-to-build-the-perfect-team.html. Accessed August 14, 2023.

35. Cross, Rob, Reb Rebele, and Adam Grant. "Collaborative Overload." *Harvard Business Review*, January-February 2016. https://hbr.org/2016/01/collaborative-overload. Accessed August 14, 2023.

36. Gallup, Inc. *State of the Global Workplace 2022 Report.* Washington, D.C.: Gallup, Inc., 2022.

37. Peck, Rachel. "5 Ways the 'Yes, And' Improv Technique Can Help You at Work—While Protecting Your Boundaries." Well + Good Career Advice (Blog), Well + Good, March 30, 2023. https://www.wellandgood.com/yes-and-improv-technique-work/. Accessed August 14, 2023.

OTHER BOOKS AND PUBLICATIONS BY WENDY GATES CORBETT

ATD Consulting Handbook (contributing author, coming in 2024)

ATD Handbook for Training and Talent Development (contributing author)

Five Questions for Great Presentation Visuals

101 Ways to Make Learning Active Beyond the Classroom (contributing author)

101 More Ways to Make Training Active (contributing author)

SCORE! For Webinar Training, Volume 5 (contributing author)

Designing for the Virtual Classroom

Simple Effective Online Training

ABOUT THE AUTHOR

 Belonging is a central part of Wendy Gates Corbett's life. Her research on belonging began the day she was born as a biracial child adopted into a white family. As an organizational consultant, Wendy works with employees and leaders at all levels to create thriving workplace communities where employees are seen, heard, and valued. As a global keynote speaker and certified trainer, Wendy has trained over 150,000 people around the world. She is an adjunct professor of management and leadership at Duke University. Wendy serves as a member of the board of trustees of Guilford College, her undergraduate alma mater.

Wendy works with organizations in a variety of ways, including:

- Executive consulting with leaders to identify focus areas and strategies for strengthening the sense of belonging
- Participating in strategic leadership summits
- Administering the *Belonging at Work Survey*© and identifying strengths and challenge areas
- Hosting kickoff events for employee resource groups (ERGs) and ERG leaders
- Speaking at DEI-related conferences and events
- Consulting with and providing training for leaders and employees

To learn more, visit wendygatescorbett.com or reach out to Wendy on LinkedIn.

Made in the USA
Columbia, SC
19 July 2024

38985819R00095